It's probably some dark fault in my own character, but I've never been much for reading biographies, especially missionary biographies. I suppose that I suspect most of them are, to some extent, hagiography. But this is a reliable narrative by a good writer. He tells the story well and it's not the success story most expect from such a tale. The final chapter, with its recommendations, is a gem by itself. But those recommendations make best sense in the context of the whole story that precedes them. This is a tale well worth reading in part because it's contemporary. It demonstrates all the benefits and all the pitfalls of modern mission work: the ability to be on the field in less than a day (as opposed to weeks), but also the dangers and frustrations of working in a country antagonistic to the gospel. Welcome to the real world of modern missions.

BEN SHAW
Professor of Old Testament, Reformation Bible College

This page-turning account of God calling one family to serve in an extraordinary way will open your eyes to both the darkness and gospel opportunity in foreign lands. Read on and be encouraged that God is doing great things through his people, and wonder if the next unlikely person might be you!

PAT DALY
Vice President, Greenville Presbyterian Theological Seminary

This honest account of a brief tenure in a foreign missions field contains well-told stories of hope and joy amid enormous challenges, dangers, and disappointments, but minus the triumphalism that often accompanies missionary tales. The fullness of God's grace produces surprising fruit when crises become ministry opportunities, barriers turn into blessings, and isolated conditions yield unexpected occasions for fellowship. Beyond its value for individuals (and especially families) considering a missionary calling, this book will, for all readers, expand their understanding of and enrich their prayers for the worldwide mission of the church.

Dean of Libraries
Reformed

A compelling read. The writer's honesty, passion and struggles are refreshing, including ways in which he and his wife responded in situations. The book should be essential reading for all missionary candidates but also for church/mission leaders, especially in not rushing the process. You will benefit from reading this excellent book!

D. ERYL DAVIES

Research Supervisor, Union School of Theology, Bridgend, Wales, author, *No Difficulties with God: The Life of Thomas Charles, Bala (1755-1814)*

THE MOST UNLIKELY MISSIONARIES

Serving God's Kingdom in the Middle Kingdom

住在中国服侍神国

J. M. Gurvsy

CHRISTIAN
FOCUS

Copyright © J.M. Gurvsy 2023

paperback ISBN 978-1-5271-0989-6
ebook ISBN 978-1-5271-1034-2

10 9 8 7 6 5 4 3 2 1

Published in 2023
by
Christian Focus Publications Ltd,
Geanies House, Fearn, Ross-shire,
IV20 1TW, Great Britain.

www.christianfocus.com

Cover design by Daniel van Straaten

Printed and bound by
Bell & Bain, Glasgow

Contents

*To those who sacrificed to send and support us:
though God's purposes may remain forever veiled,
your labors in the Lord are never in vain.*

Foreword

Being a disciple of Jesus Christ carries a cost. Some of the costs which those contemplating missionary service in another land must consider include the loss of: in-person contact with your family, especially your parents (who are also the grandparents of your children), long-time friends, and dear brothers and sisters in Christ; competency in the local language and in the customs of the local culture (and how that affects your participation in gatherings for public worship); and the ability to go out in public without immediately drawing attention to yourself because you look so different from those all around you. (I still remember visiting our missionaries in China more than a quarter of a century ago and, as we walked down the street, having the local children gather around us, gleefully pointing and laughing at our noses because they were so big! In fact, I was told that one of their nicknames for Westerners was "big noses.") Yet even as Christ reveals to those who would be His disciples the real cost of that discipleship – renouncing all (Luke 14:33) – He also promises them that those who have given up all for the sake of the kingdom of God will receive many times more in this life, and in the age to come, eternal life (Luke 18:30).

This refreshing little volume is the story of a loving husband and wife in their thirties and a few years into their first pastorate in a university town that was bearing good fruit, who decided to leave all behind and, with their five children, be sent by their church to the land of China (the Middle Kingdom) to work with the developing church there. With a humble transparency, the author shares with us the couple's joys and struggles along the way, taking particular delight in being able to discern ways in which God, in His divine providence, has ordered life events in the past in order to prepare them for the present (and the future, too).

Although their time on the mission field was relatively brief, less than two years, they were in Chengdu when the massive government crackdown on Early Rain Covenant Church, with which the mission was working, resulted in scores of arrests of church leaders and the expulsion of most of their mission team. They persevered, despite the new loneliness arising from the loss of their closest partners in the team, learning afresh to love the Lord, not just for the gifts He gives us, but simply for Himself.

Each week while they were on the field, they would send a newsletter to those back in the States who were upholding them in prayer. There would be a total of one hundred such newsletters, which, together with the author's private journals, would provide much of the background for a considerable amount of this book's contents. As you read these pages, my prayer is that your hearts will again be warmed towards Christ, and that you will be able to exclaim with the author: Jesus is worth it!

M. T. "Barnabas"

Introduction

The Chinese word for China is *Zhōngguó* – literally the "Middle Kingdom." The name is approximately three thousand years old. It bears a twofold witness to China's self-understanding. In a geographic sense, China sees itself as the "middle" of the world. Whereas world maps produced in the West often place Europe and Africa at the center along the "Prime Meridian," in China it is not strange to see world maps with China at the center.

China also sees itself as the "Middle Kingdom" in a cultural sense. The Chinese are an ancient people with a colorful history and impressive legacy. Remains of human settlement stretch back more than five thousand years, and ancient China produced "Four Great Inventions" that shaped the course of global civilization: the compass, gunpowder, papermaking, and printing. I have stood on walls in China that were "new" several centuries before Europeans discovered the New World. The famous "Terracotta Army" was buried two centuries before the birth of Christ. The first Christian missionaries came to China in AD 635.

Our family landed in China just a few days after North Korea tested its hydrogen bomb in 2017. We left China in 2019, just a few months before the COVID-19 outbreak. In total, we served in China for slightly less than two years. What eventful years they turned out to be.

In the same month that we arrived, the Chinese government officially reversed a nearly forty-year trend of gradually easing its restrictions on religious activities. New regulations were issued and went into effect on 1 February, 2018. Ten months later, on 9 December, 2018, police raided Early Rain Covenant Church in Chengdu (southwest China), arresting more than 100 people and seizing all the property of the church and its seminary. We were living in Chengdu at that time, serving on a team with connections to both institutions.

We returned to North America in late spring 2019 for what we expected would be a temporary stay. By summer, when it became clear that our family would not return to China, our hearts were a mix of emotions. On one hand, there was some obvious relief. Despite its exotic charms, life for a large clan in a country geared toward small families presented many emotional and logistical challenges. Then there was the language barrier.

On the other hand, we had given our lives to China. The need was as large as China's enormous population, the opportunities as rich as her culture and history. Many people had made great sacrifices, and committed significant resources, to get us to the far side of the world. Just under two years into what we expected would be at least two decades, we were beginning to hit our stride with the language and with life rhythms. We had connections with Chinese Christians. We helped newcomers get settled, hosted foreign visitors, and occasionally served as impromptu tour guides. To crown it all, we had even found a scouting troop for our sons. How could all of it be over so soon, and so suddenly?

For these reasons, there was another emotional side to our departure from China. Beyond the outward relief, there was an inward sense of profound discouragement. Why had God done this? Why ask us to leave everything and everyone behind (you try taking five grandchildren away from three sets of grandparents), undergo all the difficulties of a cross-cultural transition, bear all the stress of living as a missionary family in a closed country, and invest all the hours in learning one of the world's most challenging languages… only to pull the rug out from under us just when we were learning to walk?

Within the first weeks of our reentry to North American culture, we encountered many well-meaning people who would say things like, "I bet you're glad to be back!" or "Welcome home!" These were hard words to bear. Having taught ourselves that home was not where we were born, but where God called us to live, and having followed God's clear leading to a different home... how could it be so simple? Our friends did not understand.

Yet as the weeks wore on, we began to encounter another regular response: people who thanked us for the weekly letters we had written (100 in total) during our time of service. These weekly letters, containing a mix of cultural observations, family narrative, and theological reflection, proved to have been a surprising encouragement to many readers. One reader was so careful in printing and archiving our letters that he even noticed when we accidentally skipped a digit in our numbering scheme.

The present work has arisen partly in response to this encouragement. For alongside the weekly updates, we also wrote hundreds of personal letters to friends and family – often containing anecdotes and details that went well beyond the "public" letters. For matters too sensitive even for personal letters, my wife and I kept private journals. In total, the raw story of our two years in China amounts to more than 270,000 words. The formal goal of the present work is to distill this mass of occasional information into a coherent narrative.

But the primary purposes of the present work are far more human. First, as those who love good stories in general, we want to share ours. Second, as those who have received much encouragement from missionary stories in particular, we want to try to encourage others: those who may someday be called by Christ to take the cross abroad, and all the rest of us who are called to send and support them. Finally, the process of telling one's story is often the pathway to perspective. In telling our story to others, we will also remind ourselves: no matter where He leads or what He asks, Jesus is worth it.

Readers may be surprised at the significant portion of this book given to events preceding our departure for China: our initial call into ministry, our early years of service as church planters, and finally the long sequence of events that took us abroad. Why include all this? There are two reasons. The first is simply a matter of fact: as any missionary can testify, the sacrifice and struggles begin long before one steps on a plane.

Our family spent just under two years living in China, but China was living in us for the entire year we spent preparing ourselves, our family and friends, and our church for our departure.

The second reason is closely related to the first: too many missionary biographies abbreviate or omit altogether the "backstory." We believe this is a significant mistake, for Jesus commands us to "count the cost," (Luke 14:28). Our hope is that in recounting what following Him to China cost us, we will encourage and equip future missionaries – and those who send them – to do the same.

Caveat:
Regarding Memory, Names, and Security

The events and facts in this story are all, to the best of our memory, accurately recounted and faithfully related. Yet memories are not flawless, especially when it comes to the exact words of old conversations. Reconstructed dialogues in the following account, therefore, should be regarded more like "inspired summaries" than verbatim transcripts. Similarly, quotations from our public and private letters have, at points, been lightly edited for the sake of concision, clarity, or security.

Regarding security, three things must be noted:

1. Regarding our time in China, some names have been deliberately altered and other details intentionally obscured. This is done not to embellish the truth or massage the facts, but rather to protect the identities of persons and places where missionary activity remains ongoing – or in order to protect the identities and ministries of national partners. For example, I have intentionally concealed the names of the province, city, and school where I served in northeast China – referring to our location simply as "Dongbei" ("the Northeast").

2. I have applied similar cloaking to certain aspects of our life and movements before China, as seemed prudent in order to prevent backtracking through association with

our real identities. For example, I never reveal the name of the city, the congregation, or the denomination in which we ministered in Pennsylvania prior to accepting the call to missionary service.

3. I write under a pseudonym. I received the name "Gurvsy" from the children of an old friend. Imagination supplied the rest.

Context:
Five Key Events in the History of Chinese Missions

Every time I have been given the opportunity to speak about our work in China, I begin by presenting five key events from Chinese missions history. Though no shortlist can possibly encapsulate the entire picture, I have found that familiarity with the following five events provided our audience with a useful frame of reference – however basic and incomplete – for beginning to understand the modern Chinese missionary context. By including them here, I hope that readers of this memoir will benefit similarly.

In 1807, Robert Morrison arrived as the first Protestant missionary to China. Sent out by the London Missionary Society, Morrison faced daunting prospects even to make a beginning. At that time, foreigners were permitted no permanent residence in China. It was a capital crime for any Chinese to teach their language to a foreigner. Nevertheless, Morrison succeeded in learning the language, writing the first Chinese-English dictionary, and producing the first complete Chinese translation of the Bible.[1]

---

1. For more information, see Christopher Hancock, *Robert Morrison and the Birth of Chinese Protestantism* (London: T&T Clark, 2008).

The second event occurred in 1839, when Great Britain launched the first "Opium War" in order to force China to permit British merchants to sell opium to the Chinese population. British victory in 1842 began China's "century of humiliation," as foreign governments – eventually including the United States – forced China to sign a series of "unequal treaties." Japanese invasion, occupation, and depredations in China during the Second World War (1937–1945) only exacerbated this humiliation and resentment of foreign imperialism. To this day, Chinese prickliness toward "foreign interference" can be traced to these years.

The third event occurred in 1949, when Communist victory in the Chinese Civil War established the People's Republic of China under Mao Zedong. Within the next few years, Communist authorities expelled all foreign missionaries. Anti-Christian sentiment reached its peak during the Cultural Revolution (1966–1976): churches were closed, and believers buried their Bibles in order to protect them from destruction.[2]

The fourth event occurred in 1978, when Deng Xiaoping became China's "paramount leader" after the death of Mao Zedong. Deng launched a new campaign of "reform and opening," transforming China's economy from a disaster of central planning into an Asian tiger using a capitalistic, "socialist market economy." As part of this campaign, state-approved "registered" Christian churches were restored and reopened for worship in 1979.

The fifth event is much more recent. In 2012, Xi Jinping became the new "core leader" of China. From the outset of his premiership, one of Xi's signature initiatives was an "anti-corruption" campaign that removed many potential political rivals. Having done this, Xi's began his second term with constitutional revision. His personal ideology, "Xi Jinping Thought," was officially made part of the Constitution of the Chinese Communist Party in 2017. The next year, Xi succeeded in removing the two-term limit on his stay in power.

Xi Jinping is a nationalist. In China it is sometimes heard, "Mao made China stand up; Deng made China rich; Xi will make China

---

2. For more information on the formative years of Chinese Christianity under revolutionary China, see David Aikman, *Jesus in Beijing* (Washington, DC: Regnery, 2006).

strong." Xi's domestic policy includes a significant increase of censorship and surveillance – such as the stern new regulations regarding "illegal" religious groups. Abroad, Xi's ambitious "One Belt One Road" plan invokes memories of the ancient Silk Road as it seeks to establish land and sea trade corridors extending from Beijing into Africa and Europe.

So what was God doing through these five key events in Chinese missions history?

In the years between Robert Morrison and Mao Zedong (1807–1949), the Lord used foreign missionaries to plant the Chinese Church and produce the first complete Chinese Bible. During this period, many Christian workers made use of their foreign status and legal protections under the "unequal treaties" to advance their mission. This had the unintended consequence of creating a long-term association between Christianity and abusive foreign imperialism – with tragic consequences. In 1900, the "Boxer Rebellion" killed thousands of Chinese Christians and more than a hundred foreign missionaries. To this day, Chinese authorities continue to label foreign missionaries as "religious spies."

While originally hailed as the death of Christianity in China by Western observers, Communist expulsion of foreign missionaries in the early 1950s actually protected the Chinese Church from the influence of Western liberal theology – and put leadership of the Chinese Church into the hands of indigenous Christians. Under the blessing of God's Spirit, this produced prodigious growth: whereas there were approximately one million Chinese Christians in 1949,[3] today there are between 60-80 million. Put another way: for every year of Communist rule there are approximately 1 million new Christians in China. For this reason some have called Mao Zedong the greatest "evangelist" in Chinese history!

In the years following Mao's death (1976–2020), Deng's "reform and opening" led to mass urbanization and meteoric economic development. This has created many opportunities for the gospel among those displaced or disoriented by the rapid pace of change. This period has also seen the resumption of

---

3. For other interesting statistics, see G. Thompson Brown, *Earthen Vessels and Transcendent Power: American Presbyterians in China, 1837-1952* (New York: Orbis, 1997).

legal publication of the Bible – with millions of copies printed and distributed in China since the late 1980s. For a time, Chinese Christians could even buy the Bible online. Though now curtailed, this fact is indicative of the change China has experienced within a single generation.

Although state-approved churches reopened in 1979, they never won the full loyalty of Chinese believers. Today, more than half of China's Christians worship in unregistered "house churches." Under Xi Jinping, there are rumors of a "reduce to zero" plan intended to eliminate all such "illegal" churches. Though the effects of such a plan remain to be seen, the outcome is not uncertain. "The church is an anvil which has worn out many hammers."

Prologue:
Detained at the Border

It was one of the most existential moments of my life.

There I was, standing on a walkway looking east across the frozen Yalu River. Across that river – it could not have been a distance greater than 100 yards at the point we visited – were a collection of beautifully built, coral-colored apartment buildings. They looked almost new... but something wasn't quite right. It was February, yet no smoke was rising from the chimneys of that shiny domestic complex. Why not?

Because nobody lived there. The real homes, which we saw later from a hillside overlooking the river, were tucked behind the new apartment blocks. They were much more modest and reminded me of prison camp bunkhouses. The fabulous new buildings in front were merely a façade, meant to impress those looking across the river at ground level.

Welcome to the Asian concept of "saving face" – what the Chinese call *miànzi.*

But it was not the Chinese who had constructed this elaborate ruse for the sake of impressing those looking into their country from across the river. The empty apartment buildings stood on the North Korean side of the river. Behind the apartments, the hills were brown and had been stripped bare. We were told this was not just a phenomenon of the winter season, but the result of people desperate for any scrap of fuel they could scavenge.

So there I was: a bumpkin from the hills of central Pennsylvania, standing on the border with North Korea, staring into the barren face of what a friend once called "the world's largest prison camp," and feeling so thankful to God that I was on the "safe" side of the river... in the People's Republic of China! How did I ever get here?

My wife and I were visiting China as part of the process of discerning whether the Lord was calling our family to live and labor in the Middle Kingdom. In the course of this visit, one of our hosts had suggested taking us to see the North Korean border. It seemed like a tremendous opportunity. Little did we know it was about to go pear-shaped.

After viewing the border, both from the ground and from a nearby hill – from which vantage we could also see armed guards and earthen gravemounds along the eastern riverbank – we got back into our car to return. We were supposed to fly to another city that very afternoon, so all of our luggage was in the boot of the car. Yet in order to maximize our opportunity to see and pray for North Korea, our driver had been instructed to take the road that paralleled the course of the Yalu River. For a short while, things went as planned.

Then we hit the checkpoint.

Most of the cars, carrying only Chinese citizens, were waved through after only a brief stop. But when our car pulled up, containing a Chinese driver and three foreigners – my wife, myself, and one of our friends – we must have triggered some sort of security protocol. The soldiers were neither impolite nor threatening, but they were firm. They wanted to see our passports. They wanted to know what we were doing. Even after we told them we were tourists, they wanted to know our occupations.

For our friend and for my wife, the answer to the last question was simple enough. The former was a teacher, the latter was a full-time mother. Then it came to me.

"I am a teacher," I said. It was an obfuscation I had learned from reading Brother Andrew's book, *God's Smuggler*. And it was true: as a pastor in Pennsylvania, my primary duty was teaching the Bible. I could give this answer with a clear conscience.

The follow-up question, however, was more difficult.

"What subject do you teach?"

Although I had another answer ready – "Ancient Near Eastern Literature," a tip I had picked up from a colleague with overseas experience – I never needed to use it, because in that moment our friend spoke up.

"Don't you also teach English?"

It was true. Besides my work as a pastor, I had also taught English grammar and composition for the last two years in Pennsylvania as a tutor with Classical Conversations. Not only was this answer true, it was also less likely to attract further follow-up. Foreigners who taught English were not rare birds in China.

With this answer, the questioning more or less subsided – but our passports were not returned. Instead, we were made to wait while the soldiers completed their protocol. We were brought bottled water, and the soldiers proceeded to unload and unpack our luggage. Although somewhat invasive, this was not overly alarming. Our luggage did not contain anything controversial.

I was, however, becoming increasingly afraid that we might be asked to step out of the car – and that if so, the soldiers might see the shoulder bag which I had so far kept hidden under my feet in the front seat. Were they to discover that bag, and sift carefully through its contents, there would definitely be trouble. For inside my bag, carefully folded and tucked into the inner pocket of a portfolio case, were all the sensitive papers my potential colleague had been handing me throughout the time of our stay. These included a list of Christian books available for distribution, as well as a set of meeting minutes for a local underground church. The papers were bilingual, meaning there would be no difficulty for the authorities to understand them. What would happen if these were discovered?

After about an hour, just as things appeared to be winding down at the checkpoint, we saw a white van approach – the Public Security Bureau (Chinese police).

"Please tell me this isn't for us," said our friend.

But we all knew it was.

Thankfully, we were not made to ride in the white van. Instead, our driver was ordered to follow the police back along the river road to their local station. Once there, our passports once again disappeared inside for the grand tour and our baggage was again unpacked and inspected. The officers were amused to find us transporting chocolate, and we were made to wait another hour while the police followed their protocols.

During this wait, our driver must have thought that his foreign guests were in need of entertainment. Lucky for us, his car came equipped with a television – and even luckier, he was able to connect to a channel playing music videos.

And so it was that on a cold day in February, on the far side of the world, detained by Chinese police along the border with North Korea... we found ourselves quite literally a "captive audience" to the music videos of Justin Bieber.

I am not joking.

In the end, the police never made us get out of the car – and they never found my bag.

They repacked our luggage, returned our passports, and asked to look at the photos on our phone. Having assured them that we had taken no pictures beyond the usual tourist sort, they let us go – but made our driver turn around and return by another way. When we asked our driver why, his reply was difficult to understand – but apparently foreigners were no longer permitted on the river road.

Sometime later, as we debriefed over coffee and the tension faded, we were enabled to see both the humor and the advantage of this encounter. After all, if we were really going to live and serve in China, then we would face the real possibility of being detained by the authorities – for any reason, or for no reason at all. And if you might be detained at any time during your stay... why not have a trial run the first time you visit?

The fact that the Lord used this early experience to give us perspective, rather than send us packing, is itself an indicator of how God had already begun to change us. Right from the outset, He was showing us that life overseas would not be all sunshine and lollipops. In helping us thus to count the cost, He drew us to a deeper sense of His supreme worth.

Ultimately, this is what sustains a missionary in their life and labors abroad – an abiding, living sense that Jesus is worth whatever He asks, because only He gives true life. The world defines life in terms of what cannot be kept: beauty, health, wealth, etc. Jesus defines life not by what cannot be kept, but by what cannot be lost. As missionary martyr Jim Elliot famously said, "He is no fool who gives what he cannot keep to gain what he cannot lose."

On that cold February day on the border of North Korea, we took a small step in learning this lesson. There would be many more to come.

Chapter 1:
The Most Unlikely Missionaries

When we were growing up, if you had told either my wife or myself that our family would someday serve as missionaries in China, we would never have believed you. We were reared in the rural center of Pennsylvania where the landscape is old, the lifestyle is slow, and the most colorful thing you will ever see are the leaves in autumn. In childhood, the closest I ever came to anything Chinese were the illegal fireworks purchased by my uncle for the Fourth of July – and the occasional drive past the Chinese restaurant where we never ate.

I share this not to criticize my home or its people, but rather to emphasize an important point: there is simply no way of telling whom God might call to serve Him abroad. Some missionaries sense God's hand on their life from a young age. Others find themselves drawn more slowly, by gentle steps, until one day you round a corner of the path... and find yourself in a different country. Our road to China was definitely of the latter type.

My wife and I met through the internet when we were seventeen years old, during our junior year of high school. Though we only lived four miles apart, we lived in different school districts, and so our lives had never intersected. Thank God, we found each other through a mutual interest in Christian punk rock music – and within six months we knew that we wanted to be married. Our parents, however, insisted that we finish college (and high school) first. So that is what we did: after our senior years of high school, we took university classes year-round and finished in three years. We graduated one Saturday, and got married the next. It was all a happy whirlwind.

It should be noted at this point that, while we were serious about Jesus and the church, we did not perceive any call toward pastoral ministry. During high school we had both read C.S. Lewis, and during university this had developed for me into a significant interest in philosophy. Alongside of my Computer Science major and Mathematics minor, I picked up a second minor in Philosophy. I applied, and was even accepted into, a doctoral program in Philosophy. In the end, however, due to some peculiar providence, we did not go on to graduate school. I took a job as a software engineer, we bought a house, and began a family.

For a few years, life seemed simple. Then my heart began to itch.

The dissatisfaction did not stem from anything at work or at home. I was successful in my career, we were happily married, and God had given us our first son. On the surface, everything was excellent. Yet I could not escape the sense that there was something more. Looking back, I think it's probably safe to say that some part of this was selfish ambition and youthful arrogance. But I think, too, that there was another part.

From my early years, I have carried in my heart a concern for people's souls. Though I have never been a tremendous witness for Christ, nor boldly outgoing, I have always wondered whether the people in my life – especially close family, friends, and co-workers – were ready to die. When given the opportunity, I enjoyed discussing these deeper issues of life and destiny. In fact, I liked it even more than I enjoyed writing software. This being the case, it seemed like an honest question: did God have other plans for us?

As it turned out, He did. Little by little, He began to pull us away from a comfortable engineering life and out into the wider, wilder work of His kingdom. In the wake of this first itch, I began taking part-time classes and came under the oversight of our "presbytery" – a regional group of churches. While continuing to work as an engineer, I took a job with a software company in southern California. In this position I began to interact with many internationals, both clients and coworkers. Though I had a lush "work from home" job in the days when such things were yet rare, I traveled to Los Angeles at least a half-dozen times each year – thus becoming acquainted with urban life. God was peeling back the cover, slowing revealing glimpses of the life He would someday have for us.

The big change came in 2008. At that point, my wife and I had come to a major decision point. Our family was growing and my job was only going to get busier. I had completed a few seminary courses as a part-time student, but at the current rate it was going to take me nearly a decade to finish even a two-year theological degree. In the meantime, we were thinking about a third baby. I didn't think there was enough room in my head to continue as a full-time husband, father, engineer – and also as a part-time seminarian. Something had to give, and seminary was the only thing that we felt we could responsibly drop.

Our church leadership, however, thought differently. Sensing God's call on our life and desiring us to continue in training, they took the extraordinary step of offering me a newly created "pastoral assistant" position. This position provided a modest salary, medical insurance, and full seminary tuition. Though we hesitated at first, especially regarding the gap between a software versus a seminarian salary, my wife and I finally decided to accept. Thus I left engineering and entered full-time ministry.

At the time they hired me, our church envisioned a future where I would finish training and then continue with them as an associate pastor. This was a perfectly acceptable plan to our family, and we gave no thought to alternatives. Then God intervened again.

In 2010, our church took on oversight for a new church plant in a neighboring city. This city was home to one of Pennsylvania's most important research universities. Our pastor was not eager to lose his intern and future associate, and the elders had a different man in mind to serve as the church planter. Nevertheless, my pastor told me early on that he could see how my engineering background and interests in philosophy might be a good fit. He said something like, "We don't have any plans to send you there... but don't rule it out."

As it happened, this was good advice – for by the middle of 2011, the plans changed. The original candidate for the new church decided not to move forward, and so I was appointed to be the church planter. By the end of the year, my wife and I, along with our four sons, had left the prospect of a stable associate pastorate and stepped out of the boat onto the uncertain seas of church planting.

Life and ministry in a central Pennsylvania college town turned out to be a good fit for us. The international flavor I had come to enjoy in my second engineering job was everywhere – more than half the nations of the world had students studying at our university. Within a few months, I had begun volunteering with an on-campus ministry serving international students. Over the course of the next few years, we would host people in our home from Turkey, the Netherlands, even Iran. Once I was even given the privilege to come and explain the Easter holiday to an ESL class composed almost entirely of Saudi Arabian students. As a long-time international ministries veteran put it: in this place, the "nations were on our doorstep."

Beyond this exotic element, the folks with whom we labored to form a new church were an amazing group of people: flexible, sacrificial, talented, and teachable. Though many had come from existing congregations in the city, they were genuinely eager to plant a church that would reach lost souls. Not only were they eager for the new church to succeed, they were anxious in the proper sense for their new pastor and his young family to thrive. They loved us, encouraged us, and supported us well. I remember many times during those early years seeing other pastors post horror stories on social media. I simply could not relate. We had a wonderful relationship with our people.

Over the next several years, the Lord did exciting things through our new congregation in the university city. A ninety-four year old man confessed his sins to Jesus and began a new life; exactly two months later, on Christmas morning, he died and entered heaven. A college freshman we met through our on-campus open-air ministry was also wonderfully converted. Other students attended faithfully, and lapsed Christians who had drifted away from various churches found a new home with us. Our membership included people who had spent time in prison, and one woman – a lady who had struggled for years with assurance – came to me after one service saying, "Pastor, I don't know what's happening to me. Lately I've just been filled with a sense... that God loves me!"

This isn't to say we never had struggles. Every church does, and a university city is hard soil for the Christian message. Nevertheless, both my wife and I felt that we had been given a real plum of a church to serve. Our people were engaged, the Spirit was at work, and the congregation grew from a core group of less than twenty to a worshiping community of approximately seventy. Less than three years after my ordination, our church "particularized": the congregation elected four elders and voted unanimously to call me to continue as their pastor. It was one of the happiest days of our ministry.

The same year that the church particularized, our family purchased a home in the community. After many years in transition, it seemed to us that we were dropping the anchor at last. We would serve this church and this city for the rest of my ministry. I would shepherd these people from cradle to grave – until the day that I was buried beside them. Our kids had a big back yard with a (leaky) swimming pool and a custom-built treehouse. What more could we possibly want?

There was only one problem with this wonderful plan. Though we talked about it with others, we never actually submitted it to God. Of course He would agree, right?

Chapter 2:
A Dangerous Prayer

I ran my first marathon in our first year of church planting. Over the next few years, I ran another full marathon and a handful of half marathons. Long-distance jogging was not only how I got my exercise; it was also how I did the lion's share of my reading.

In the autumn of 2014, my jogging soundtrack was a book by Philip Jenkins, *The Next Christendom*.[1] For those who aren't familiar with this work, it is a meticulously researched monograph detailing the explosion of Christianity in the global East and South. Though the book was more than ten years old by the time I first encountered it, the following year (2015) I had the chance to meet Dr. Jenkins. That conversation confirmed to me that the trends he had documented were continuing, or perhaps even increasing.

It is hard to overstate just how much of an encouragement it was to me, as a pastor regularly facing the apathy of Western secularism, to have the details of Jenkins's findings wash over me as the miles passed beneath my feet. Yes, the tide of gospel light might be receding in North America and Europe, but globally speaking, the goodness of Jesus was spreading like a tsunami.

---

1. Philip Jenkins, *The Next Christendom: The Coming of Global Christianity*, 3rd ed. (New York: OUP, 2011).

This newborn interest in global Christian movements began to grow. I found and read other books. I began to see that we who believe in Jesus have more in common with Christians in China or Iran than we do with our non-Christian neighbors across the street. I learned that the apostle Peter used racial terms like *genos* and *ethnos* when speaking of the church (see 1 Peter 2:9). I thereby realized that, as believers, our primary ethnicity is not American but Christian – and therefore we have a duty to identify with the global church more than we identify with any nation on earth.

This was exciting stuff. As it sunk into my own heart, I began sharing it with my family – and preaching it to our congregation. Taking this truth to heart, members of our congregation stepped up and provided hospitality meals to newly arrived international students. A couple of families – including our own – even volunteered to host Chinese children in their homes for a week during the summer.

Nothing seemed particularly unusual in any of this. Indeed, it all just seemed like the church doing what a church should do: identifying the opportunities for the gospel in its community, and then stepping in to supply the need. Little did we know, all of these things were but the prelude to a much larger providential intervention.

Though I did not realize it at the time, a decisive moment came in June 2015. I had been elected as a commissioner to the national "General Assembly" of our denomination, and so when summer came around we piled the whole family into our minivan and hit the road. By this time, "our whole family" had grown to seven; a few years back, the Lord had added a little girl to our squad of boys. The trip to the hinterlands of the American midwest for General Assembly would be the longest journey we had ever made together.

Though that particular General Assembly would have its share of controversy, there was no conflict among the commissioners when our foreign missionaries reported. It was a quiet summer night, and most of us listened attentively as "Robert" ("Rob" for short), a missionary to China, gave his report on what God was doing through his labors. For me, who had lately grown so interested in this global work – including the work of Robert in particular, some of whose writing I had read – it was a particular privilege.

The fateful moment came at the end of the presentation, when Rob implored the Assembly to "pray for young men who would be willing to learn the language and give their lives to China." This being a reasonable enough request, I immediately began to pray that the Lord would indeed raise up such men. But as I prayed, I began to feel a bit awkward. Could I, a younger man, in good conscience ask the Lord to raise up and send others... if I was not willing, even hypothetically, to volunteer myself?

Convicted by this, I modified my prayer. "Lord, I don't see how it could ever be possible," – though our church plant had particularized, it was still so young – "but if You want, I'd go... Amen."

Just like that, I had offered the single most dangerous prayer of our lives.

Something in me realized this, too. "If I tell my wife about it, she'll think I'm crazy." There had been times in our early married life when I had toyed with big, life-changing ideas and caused my better half serious alarm. I could only too easily predict what she would say to this. Sitting beside me at the Assembly that summer – even that very night – was also one of the elders from our church in Pennsylvania. I did not mention to him what I had prayed, either. In fact, there was something so impulsive and outlandish about the whole idea that I decided it would be better not to speak of it at all – to anybody.

And here's where the story takes a particularly interesting twist. Because I never spoke about this prayer, I forgot about it completely. Given what followed, it seems preposterous to suggest... but it truly was as if the Lord hid the memory from my own heart. To the best of my knowledge, it did not resurface for almost ten months – by which time other pieces had been set in motion.

Returning home from General Assembly, my family faced a busy few weeks. Besides resuming my duties at the church, those Chinese boys we had volunteered to host – from some city in southwest China we had never heard of, a place called "Chengdu" – were on our doorstep within a month. The day after they left our home, we were back in the van on the road again – this time to a family vacation at the beach.

To understand what happened next, one needs to understand that at this point – four years into my first pastoral call – I was perhaps on a trajectory toward burnout. Not only was I the only pastor, I was also the clerk of our "session" (the board of elders), the marketing department, the secretary, and webmaster. On top of this, I also served as the moderator of our presbytery. One of our elders was concerned I was too busy. So was my wife.

So as we sat down for some private time during our beach vacation, one of the things my beloved and I discussed was what we could do to make sure I did something other than work. As we brainstormed together, my mind went back to a friend I had known in seminary – a brother from Brazil who not only attended seminary classes in English, but whom I had seen teaching himself Latin on the side. Thinking of this, I had an idea.

"Why don't we learn a foreign language as a family?" I suggested. From the time I had first read the works of J.R.R. Tolkien as a teenager, I had been fascinated by language. During high school and college, I had dabbled in almost half a dozen: Spanish, French, Latin, Scots Gaelic, and German. My wife had studied French in college, and had done well. But neither of us had ever studied a spoken language to point of acquiring proficiency beyond what was required in the classroom.

The idea of learning a foreign language also fit with our family's interest in global Christian movements. As we thought of which languages might be most useful, we came up with a short list. The three most-spoken, important languages in the world were clearly English, Spanish, and Chinese. If you could speak those languages, you could go almost anywhere and find somebody with whom you could converse. Why not learn one of these languages together, as a family? Not only would we have our own private "code language," which would be fun for our clan, but then perhaps someday we or our children could travel and meet Christians in other parts of the world.

But which language to choose? Between Spanish and Mandarin, Spanish was clearly the easier choice. "But they can pick that up in college," I suggested. "When they're young is the time to give them the harder language, because it's easier to learn language as a child."

I remember sensing that we should probably pray about this idea. But we didn't. Instead, I sent a fistful of emails to people we knew looking for suggestions on how to get started learning Mandarin. And before we left the beach, my friend from international ministries in the university city had connected us with a tutor. We began our lessons the following month, in August 2015.

A year or so later, when we were asked seriously to discern whether or not we were called to leave our pastorate in Pennsylvania and move to China, this moment seemed to us highly compelling. There we were, less than a month after I had secretly offered myself to the Lord for China... and what were we doing when I sent those emails from the beach? In taking steps to engage a Mandarin tutor, my wife and I were taking the first steps toward fulfilling the prayer I had made at the General Assembly. Still, I remembered nothing.

I had forgotten my dangerous prayer. Jesus had not forgotten.

Chapter 3:
Sister Hallelujah

Almost every month of my ministry in the university city, I met for lunch with "Paul" – a dear friend, colleague, and mentor. There was never any script for our meetings; the goal was simply to bare our souls and to bear one another's burdens. When we met in August 2015, I was eager to share our news.

"Well, I have a new hobby," I said. "We've decided as a family to learn Mandarin."

"Oh really?" Paul asked. His next question surprised me. "How would you feel if the church asked you to go and serve in China?" Paul was a member of our denomination's foreign missions committee.

"No," I insisted firmly. "This is only a hobby." We had decided to learn Mandarin as recreation for our family, not in order to leave our ministry.

Paul just smiled. "Well, you just keep learning, brother. I'm going to pray about it." Later, as we prayed before concluding our time together, Paul – in his inimitable way – had the audacity to pray that the Lord would someday use us in China. I told my wife about Paul's comments later, but neither of us took them seriously. Chinese was just a hobby.

Yet as far as hobbies go, learning Mandarin is not quite as easy as taking up gardening. William Milne (1785–1822), the second Protestant missionary to China, famously stated: "Learning the Chinese language requires bodies of iron, lungs of brass, heads of oak, hands of spring steel, eyes of eagles, hearts of apostles, memories of angels, and lives of Methuselah." This testimony is true.

Thankfully, we had a wonderful tutor. "Jo" was born in northeast China, and had become a Christian during her university days in Beijing – thanks to the loving witness of American student missionaries. Before her conversion, she had attended the famous Tiananmen Square demonstrations in 1989. Though she herself was not physically wounded when the military attacked (she had a friend injured by a bullet ricochet), nevertheless the events had left an indelible impression on her. "I was not converted," she explained to us, "but I learned that I was not in control of my life." After university, she came to America for graduate studies – where she married, settled, and eventually became a citizen.

Jo was a perfect tutor for my wife and me: friendly, gifted, and patient. Her niece became the tutor for our children. In a short time, they became more than merely our teachers; they were our friends. We shared meals together, and our families celebrated holidays together.

Jo never pressured us to consider missionary service – though she later admitted that she had always held out secret hope.

The following spring (April 2016), we received an extraordinary opportunity. My in-laws were planning an international trip to China with their local chamber of commerce. Through their invitation, my wife and I could also attend – at a dramatically reduced price. In light of our budding interest in Chinese culture, history, and language, it seemed like too good of an opportunity to pass up. Besides, it had been more than eight years since we had been away from our kids together for more than one or two nights. We eagerly accepted.

Growing up in rural America in the 1980–1990s, the impression I had formed of China was heavily influenced by American patriotism, Cold War hostility, and evangelical sympathy for Chinese Christians. Putting all this together, we expected to see a country of meager prosperity, with a lot of traditional scenery, inhabited by people living in constant fear of the authorities. After all, Jo had told us about reading the Bible behind her bed curtains as a student, in order to escape detection. Moreover, as we prepared for our trip, our tour group warned us not to bring any religious literature beyond a personal Bible.

Our first journey to the Middle Kingdom was therefore truly eye-opening. In Beijing, the Great Wall and the Forbidden City showed us the antiquity, beauty, and ingenuity of Chinese culture. In Shanghai, we encountered an ultra-modern urban landscape that utterly dwarfed anything we had ever experienced in America – like a half-dozen lower Manhattans, only cleaner. Yes, there were cameras everywhere, and we regularly saw policemen mingling with the crowds – but nobody seemed afraid.

Yet the most memorable part of this trip came during our visit to Xi'an. Although not a minor city by any means, Xi'an is located deep in the Chinese interior – a fact that gives it much less of an "international" feel compared to the coastal metropolises. Xi'an is one of the oldest cities in China, and served as the capital under multiple dynasties. It was where the Silk Road began, and it was where the first Chinese emperor – Qin Shi Huang – was buried, his tomb guarded by the now world-famous Terracotta Army.

The Terracotta Army was what attracted our tour to Xi'an, and truly it did not disappoint. But about a month before we left to visit China, I had learned of another attraction housed in one of the minor museums in Xi'an: a relic known as the "Nestorian Stone." Erected in the year AD 781, this stele – a large, vertical stone slab engraved with writing – contained a record of roughly 150 years of Christian missionary activity in China during the Tang dynasty. Buried in the mid-800s, the stone was not rediscovered until the early 1600s, when its Christian connection was confirmed by Jesuit missionaries. Convinced that we might never again have the opportunity, I was determined – and was praying – that we might somehow get to see the Stone.

The opportunity came one morning when our tour guide announced that we would go to see the Wild Goose Pagoda. Having already obtained a map from our hotel, I approached our guide – whom my wife and I had gotten to know the previous day, and who was more impressed by our large family than by our fledgling Chinese – and showed her the map.

"I am a Christian," I said, "and we will probably never get to come here again." I explained that my wife and I really wanted to see the Nestorian Stone, and asked her permission for us to leave the tour for a few hours so that we could walk to the museum where it was displayed. We would rejoin the tour for supper.

"Okay," our guide said, after some initial hesitation, "but don't get lost!"

Armed with our map and our guide's mobile telephone number, we set off on what would be one of the great highlights of our trip – but not for the reason we expected.

The first challenge we faced was logistical: how does one cross a street with half a dozen lanes and half a hundred cars, bicycles, and mopeds – driven by drivers with only half-regard for the traffic laws? The problem was more daunting than it sounds; just ask my mother what it was like for her, the first time she had to cross a Chinese city street while visiting us several years later... But the solution turned out to be relatively simple. At each intersection, we simply connected ourselves to a group of Chinese pedestrians and followed their lead: stopping when they stopped – sometimes in the middle of the street! – and walking when they walked.

We found the Nestorian Stone just where it was supposed to be, and were duly impressed. To be able to see and touch a record of gospel proclamation that was a thousand years older than the earliest beginnings of one's own nation... impresses upon one the truly global and historical reality of our faith. As I would tell my students a few years later, in an underground Bible study in a different part of China, "Christianity came to your country long before it ever came to mine."

But the best part of our excursion turned out not to be the Nestorian Stone, but the living stone that we met on our walk back to join the tour. You see, there were actually two things I had prayed for regarding our trip to China: first, that we could see the Nestorian Stone; and second, that somehow we could meet Chinese Christians. Little did I know that the Lord would answer both prayers on the same afternoon.

We had first noticed the woman on our way to the museum, as we walked through the park surrounding Xi'an's ancient city walls. She was an older lady, and she had a large book open on her lap which looked a lot like a Bible. We were too nervous to speak to her the first time, but we decided we would return by the same way and, if she was still there, try to speak to her with our broken Mandarin.

Coming to the place where she still sat and read, we stopped and waited for her to look up.

Pointing to her book, we asked, *"Shèngjīng ma?"* (Bible?)

She held it up for us to see. Then, looking at us, she said, "Hallelujah?"

"Hallelujah!" we responded, surprised – but smiling – as we realized that the Chinese Bible transliterated this word for praise directly from the Hebrew, just like we do in English.

We were not able to say much more to "Sister Hallelujah" that day, but we went away that afternoon rejoicing. Not only had the Lord answered both of our prayers; He had given us our first taste of real solidarity with our global Christian family.

Chapter 4:
The Meat Hook

"So when are you moving to China?" Paul asked as we sat down for lunch a few weeks later.

Though I insisted we were not moving anywhere, Paul was gently persistent. As I reflected later on our conversation, I realized his question was not unreasonable. The Chinese Church needed experienced pastors to mentor and train them. Our denomination had openings. And here we were: a family with five years' ministry experience, interested in Chinese culture, already studying Mandarin. Shouldn't we at least consider it?

If I recall correctly, it was that same day that I finally remembered the prayer I had made during the previous year's General Assembly. The recollection brought no epiphany. It did, however, reinforce Paul's suggestion – at least somewhat.

That afternoon, I sat down with my wife and told her about Paul's question, about the need, and about the prayer. The conclusion we came to was twofold. First, we would be willing to pray about the prospect of going to China – not right away, but maybe in five to ten years. Second, if this were to be a serious consideration, then we would like to begin developing some short-term connection with our denomination's work in the field.

Having decided this together, I called Paul. I told him that we would only pray about this possibility if he also would commit to pray – and I insisted that the whole matter needed to remain confidential. He asked if he could share our potential interest with the leaders of our denominational foreign missions committee. I agreed – but nobody else was to know. A month later, I informed our church leadership that I had been asked to consider ministry in China. I also told our elders that I believed "all or nothing" was a false dichotomy, and that I simply hoped to be available for short-term work. The elders demurred.

A month or so later, as the next General Assembly was approaching – to which I had again been elected as a commissioner from my presbytery – Paul called me. He informed me that, at some point during the upcoming Assembly, I should expect to have a sidebar conversation with our foreign missions leadership. I shared this news with my wife, and we waited to see what would happen.

As it turned out, nothing happened. Although I dutifully attended the Assembly, and although I had close contact during the Assembly with our denomination's foreign missions leadership, there was never a serious conversation about our potential interest in China. The opportunities were there: in fact, at one point I was even sitting between two of our foreign missions leaders at a worship service. Before the service began, one of them looked at me and commented to the other with a smile, "Now's our chance to grab this guy and pack him off to the mission field!"

"Now's your chance," I replied. "My elder's not with me!"

I was not joking. One of the elders from our church in the university city had also been selected as a commissioner to that year's Assembly, and he had accompanied me to the worship service that morning. But as we were waiting for worship to begin, he had just stepped out to use the restroom. If ever there was a chance to speak directly, this was it.

But nothing more was said. The three of us laughed, and a few minutes later my elder returned. Worship began shortly thereafter.

I went home from the General Assembly that year feeling humbled but confused. On the one hand, the possibility that the foreign missions leaders had found other men with whom to work was a healthy check on my ego. At the same time, I was genuinely puzzled. Paul had seemed so certain that a conversation would occur. What had happened?

When next we spoke, Paul did not have the answer. We both knew that denominational leaders have a lot on their plates at any given time – and that they are especially busy during the General Assembly. Perhaps it was as simple as this. Or perhaps they indeed had found other men with whom to work. Regardless, the bottom line seemed the same: the leadership had determined not to pursue us.

As the possibility of even an exploratory connection with China faded from our attention, I also allowed the prospect to fade from our prayers. This was somewhat deliberate, for I found that keeping the prospect in mind was becoming spiritually unhealthy – if not for my wife, then at least for me. For during this time, there was a bit of tension between myself and the rest of our church leadership – and I found that it was becoming too easy to allow myself to think, "Well, if things don't go my way... I'll just go to China."

Even several years later, it is embarrassing to admit this. It was nauseatingly conceited and profoundly immature. But it also underlines the point that some possibilities are perhaps too volatile to remain on a backburner. Some prospects are simply too big to keep caged: one must either pursue or release them. In this case, we did the latter.

The summer of 2016 cooled into autumn. The tension with my elders faded, even reversed. With their support I began thinking about a ThM program. As the leaves began to change, students returned to our university city and ministry resumed its frenetic school year pace. Meanwhile, outside of pastoral labors, I was training for another race in early October – the second annual Brooklyn Half Marathon in New York City.

Beyond the fun of running with thousands of people through America's greatest city, running the Brooklyn Half was an annual opportunity to spend time visiting with my seminary classmate "Jon," who served as a pastor in Queens. We had run the inaugural race together in 2015, and were looking forward to the sequel.

After finishing the race, Jon and I had the chance to go for a drive and have a long conversation. In that conversation, he convinced me that I did not need to pursue an advanced degree. As I recall it, his reasoning was simple: we were both busy pastors, and we didn't need more degrees. He was learning Spanish, and I was learning Mandarin. That was enough extra-curricular study. Besides, if we both became fluent in our respective second languages, our local ministries could flourish in new and exciting ways.

Jon was right, and I returned from New York with renewed ministry focus and joy. Our family continued weekly Chinese lessons, but we were now convinced that any ministry connection they might have would be strictly local. We were at peace with this. In fact, we were more than at peace. Even for those few months that we had prayed about China as a long-term prospect, we had not felt any real desire to leave Pennsylvania. We loved our congregation, and we loved our community.

Now the whole matter seemed neatly resolved. We had been asked to consider, and we had prayerfully agreed. We had done our duty, and we had been passed over. No cause for shame, no need to grieve, and plenty of reason to be relieved. The whole experience had been a healthy test of our commitment to Jesus, and through it we had gained a fresh commitment to my local pastorate. There was a lot to be thankful for, and little reason to think that the matter was anything but closed. We were off the hook.

It was a Friday afternoon in late October when I received an email from "James," one of our denomination's foreign missions leaders. It was not a long communication; he simply asked if we could schedule a time to talk on the phone. James was replying to a message I had sent him a month earlier asking about Rob and his work. Earlier that year, Rob and his family had moved to Chengdu – the home city of the two Chinese boys our family had hosted the previous summer. Upon receiving this news, I had written to James, telling him that I would be praying regularly for Rob, and asking for any additional news that became available beyond official updates.

So when James called me three days later, on the last Monday in October, I thought it might very well be simply to share some extra information about Rob. In a sense, that was exactly what was going to happen... but not in any way I could have expected.

I don't remember the exact words he used, but James didn't beat around the bush.

"We want to send somebody to Chengdu to work with Rob. We'd like that to be you."

I was stunned. From everything that had happened, my wife and I both thought the China question was off the table. Now it was sitting in my lap...

So James and I talked. I explained to him that we were happy in the university city and weren't looking to leave. Yet we also believed that following Jesus involves sacrifice, and admittedly our interest and language study made us potential candidates. With much fear, therefore, I agreed to pray about the matter. But I also insisted to James that our church leadership had a clear policy: any inquiries I received from other churches or ministries had to be disclosed. I must speak with my fellow elders before taking any further steps.

Despite all these qualifications, a sense of dread settled over me as I hung up the phone – a feeling like a meat hook stuck between my ribs. I think I sensed even then that it was "all over but the crying." I was hooked. God help us. We would be moving to China.

Chapter 5:
The Cost of Discipleship

Our elders met three days later. That session meeting is etched in my memory...

The three days between James's call and the elders' meeting had not been easy for either myself or my wife. As I drove around our beloved university city, I was already beginning to feel like a ghost. And as I had contemplated how to bring this matter before our leadership, I felt caught on the horns of a dilemma.

Our elders liked to come to session meetings well-prepared. Every month, as I assembled the docket for our meetings, I would carefully prepare an agenda overview that highlighted what I felt were the most notable items we would discuss. This allowed my brothers, especially if they had minimal time, to focus their preparation on the most important items.

In this case, however, what was I to do? Should I give my men a heads-up on this? I could not imagine how to do it. On the one hand, to convey such news via email seemed to me too cold and inhuman. On the other hand, to say nothing would mean the elders would come into the discussion unprepared. I could have called them each individually – but that would have just meant having the same conversation five times, and without the benefit of being together in the same room as we processed this development.

In the end, there's just no easy way to break hard news to people you love. How do you tell the men you respect and trained, men who have supported you and shown you much grace, friends with whom you've been in the trenches of ministry for five years, brothers whom you fear to hurt and disappoint... that you might be leaving? There seemed to be no better way than to wait and share the news in-person. And so that's what I did.

Thursday evening came, and our meeting began. Routine matters of business occupied the first hour: recordings, finances, and reports on ongoing shepherding matters. During the second hour, we interviewed a candidate for membership. When we came to the place for new business at the beginning of the third hour, I spoke up.

"Brothers, at this point we need to set aside the rest of our planned docket. Something's come up that we need to discuss."

Both my words and my tone got their attention. The room got quiet.

"I received a phone call on Monday afternoon from James." Heads nodded. We all knew and liked James. He had come to our church in the past to give presentations on foreign missions work.

"As you know, the foreign missions committee has been looking for a few years to place a new family in China to work with Robert." More nods and murmurs of assent. Our church had always kept well-abreast of foreign missions news. We prayed weekly for our denomination's foreign missionaries, and from the very beginning our fledgling church had made it a priority to give funds to support spreading the gospel abroad.

"And they want us to be that family."

Dead silence.

I looked up, and the elder sitting directly across from me – a formidable man in his own field – leaned back in his chair. "Whoa," was all he said.

"As you guys know," I continued, "this is not the first time I've been asked to think about going elsewhere." They knew. I had not received many solicitations, but it had happened. "And as you know, I've always turned these down out-of-hand. My family loves it here, and we have never been looking for an exit."

More nods, but with some apprehension – as if they sensed what was coming.

"But this feels different to me," I said at last, "and I don't think I can automatically turn it down. We've agreed to pray about it, and James wants us to fill out an initial questionnaire. I told him that I would need to speak with you men first."

As the news sunk in and the initial shock receded, it was the elders' turn to surprise me.

"Well," said one brother, "I'm actually not that surprised. Once your family began learning Chinese, I started to wonder if this might happen."

Two other men nodded. "My wife and I have talked about it," said the first. The second said the same.

"I think we all thought this might happen someday," said the fourth elder – the brother seated across from me, who had by now regained his typical poise. "But we didn't expect it to happen this soon."

At this, everybody nodded – everybody except me.

Interestingly enough, the elders were sounding just like my wife. After James's call, she had said something similar. "I thought this might happen once we started learning Chinese." How had I missed it?

For the rest of the meeting that night, the other elders and I talked through the sequence of events that had brought us to this point, as well as the possibilities in moving forward. I shared with them an outline of how our interest in China had developed. They asked incisive questions and offered constructive counsel. As brothers and friends, they expressed their concerns for my wife, for our children, and for myself. As church shepherds, they clearly articulated and honestly assessed the potential impact on our congregation. As committed churchmen, they acknowledged the legitimacy of the need in China and the foreign missions committee's interest in us.

As a pastor, it was deeply gratifying to me to watch these men process together. The news had landed like a bomb, but they were handling it constructively. Although the topic was somewhat grievous, the tone was not aggrieved. Although the possibility before us would prove to be decisive in the life of the church, it did not prove divisive among the members of session. We all knew what it meant to believe and confess that Jesus is King – even if none of us had ever before been called to bend the knee to Him in such an excruciating, sacrificial way. And recognizing the gravity of the matter before us, we all understood the importance of maintaining love, respect, and unity with one another.

At this juncture, one thing that made the whole picture a bit easier to contemplate was the timetable. The proposal from the foreign missions leadership was to send us to China in autumn 2018 – almost two full years in the future. For my family, there would be time to consider well and prepare carefully. For our congregation, there would be time to process the news, erect a search committee, and provide a seamless pastoral transition. I had never looked for an exit, nor had my elders been eager to help me find one. But if this were to be, then at least we would have time to manage the changes and minimize the disruption.

Or so we thought...

Over the coming months, things would get much more difficult and tense for our session. The foreign missions committee would shift the timetable dramatically, and they would begin asking both my family and our session to embrace abrupt changes of plan and schedule. Within two months, the situation would go from feeling difficult but manageable... to feeling like things might all fall apart.

But that was in the future. On this night, despite our collective apprehension at the possibility, our session meeting concluded with sober unity. It was agreed that my wife and I should fill out the foreign missions questionnaire. It was also agreed that the matter should be kept confidential until my wife and I had reached a conclusion about our own willingness to pursue ministry in China. The elder who had spoken first with only a "whoa" now found his voice to lead us before the throne of grace. I cannot remember the words he prayed, but knowing his character I am sure that he pleaded for wisdom, and beseeched our Father in heaven to lead us – not in a way that would make us comfortable, but in a way that would make Him smile.

I went home that night with a full but heavy heart. Would we really have to leave?

Many of us have sung Luther's famous hymn, "A Mighty Fortress." Near the end of the final verse appear these words: "Let goods and kindred go, this mortal life also…" It is one thing to sing these words in memory of those who have carried the cross before us. It is quite another to sing them when the cross is before you to be carried. We were beginning to learn the real cost of discipleship.

Chapter 6:
Storm and Stress

The next month was one of our favorite holidays – American Thanksgiving. Yet this year, the normal autumn festivities were overshadowed by inner storm and stress.

With our elders now in the loop, it fell to my wife and myself to discern our calling. The two weeks after the session meeting became a season of intense prayer, reflection, and secret conversations about the opportunities and unknowns of missionary life. This was very stressful for us, because we were processing the question from very different perspectives.

I was trying to settle what I thought of as the "big questions." Was going to Asia the best use of our gifts? Did we have any biblical reasons to decline? For example, my wife had a chronic medical condition; could we get the necessary medicine and treatment for her illness in China? Regarding less significant details of day-to-day life, I was far less concerned. If the answers to the big questions led us toward China, then we would have plenty of time – and help from other missionaries – to sort out the lesser details. But if we found that answering the big questions led us away from going to China, then the lesser questions were irrelevant. Either way, it seemed to me that we must settle the big questions first, and not get bogged down in minor details.

While I was preoccupied with these principal issues, my wife focused on the practical questions. For her, one could not simply set aside questions about life logistics to focus on the "big questions." What would life look like for a family the size of ours half a world away? How would we handle the move? Where would we live? How would we go shopping without a car? Discern these clearly, she believed, and we could best discern whether we had any biblical reasons to decline a call to serve in China. Moreover, thinking through these issues in advance would help encourage her own heart – and help us answer the questions that were sure to arise from concerned family and friends.

On one fundamental matter we were both in full agreement: the discomfort and sacrifice of leaving North America did not amount to a sufficient reason to decline a call to foreign missions. Our Lord Himself had made this clear: "any one of you who does not renounce all that he has cannot be my disciple," (Luke 14:33). But beyond this point of mutual clarity, we had significant conflict. I felt that she was ignoring the big picture; she felt that I was minimizing her concerns and pressuring her to make a decision too quickly.

I should have seen then what is so clear to me now: our approaches were complementary rather than conflicting. It would have been better to wait until each of us, working from his or her own end of the pond, had met in the middle. But instead of waiting, I pressured her to decide based on my criteria before she had concluded her own deliberations. Stifling her concerns was both short-sighted and inconsiderate.

Of course, I have long since apologized to my wife. I include this matter here not because it would have changed our decision, but for two reasons. First, it is a warning to all those contemplating missionary service: the stress of a potential call can easily go before a fall. Indeed, a few years later another friend put it like this: "Going to the mission field is like pouring Miracle-Gro on sin."

Second, this incident also warns against adopting an artificial timeline. If you are not sure about a big decision, and it does not need to be decided right away, then let it wait. Think more. Pray more. Don't rush things that don't need to be rushed. This is a lesson that both my wife and I learned from our time in

China – but we wish we had understood before we ever left Pennsylvania. Foreigners will tell you: Americans are always in such a hurry.

Waiting longer would not have changed our decision to go to China, but it would have made our decision better. We should have taken more time to count the cost – a command Jesus gives immediately prior to His words about renouncing all (Luke 14:25-33). In fact, we tend to think now that there should be a mandatory, six-month minimum waiting period for all people seeking foreign missions service. Take the time to fast and pray. Take the opportunity to have long conversations with people you trust. The more a decision will change your life, the more time you should take to count the cost – and listen to your wife.

In our case, however, the whole process – from initial phone call (October 2016) to receiving the formal call from the foreign missions committee (February 2017) – took less than four months. This is a staggeringly short time to have concluded such a significant decision. Why did we move so fast?

The needs of the global church are bottomless, but the pockets of God's people are not. One of the perpetual challenges faced by every missions committee lies between these two realities: how best to allocate limited resources toward a virtually limitless need?

Yet at the end of 2016, the churches in our denomination gave extra generously toward foreign missions. In early December, I received another phone call from James. After sharing the news of this surprising increase in available foreign missions funding, he asked a question that gave me a shock: could we accelerate our timetable and consider relocating to China not in 2018, but rather 2017?

I was stunned. "I will have to talk to my wife and to our elders," I replied. "I honestly don't know what they will say."

James was understanding, and he emphasized that if 2017 could not work, then the foreign missions committee could be patient and we could continue toward the 2018 goal. Yet he emphasized that the preference on the committee's end was definitely for 2017.

"No way," said my wife flatly when I told her of the call. "There's no way we can do this." She was very unhappy, and seemed to think that I was in favor of an accelerated schedule.

I was not sure what to think. "I don't know if this is possible, but I will have to talk to the elders about it anyway. Let's just see what they say, and talk more after that."

We agreed, and the next day I wrote to our session. We had a meeting scheduled for the following week, and I did not want to blindside them again. So I shared what James had said, and tried to sketch out for them both the benefits and liabilities of an extended versus a short transition. An extended timetable (were we to leave in 2018) had the benefit of pastoral continuity and the possibility of a zero-gap transition, but it carried the liability of a "lame duck" pastor dampening the ministry of the Word. A short timetable (were we to leave in 2017) had the benefit of allowing the congregation to gain closure and pivot toward its future sooner, but carried the liability of a much greater pastoral gap.

That weekend, as our elders absorbed this latest surprise, my wife came to me with a surprising conclusion of her own: after thinking it over, she had reversed her initial reaction and come to the conclusion that an earlier transition would be better for our family. She had reached this perspective based on two facts: going sooner would mean that our family would have more time with Rob's family before their next scheduled furlough, and going sooner would also mean that our own first furlough, after four years, would coincide nicely with our eldest son's completion of high school. I had not thought of either of these things, but I was immediately convinced.

When the elders met the following Thursday, there was much more tension than in our previous discussion – despite the advanced warning. I shared with them how and why my wife and I had together concluded that an earlier transition would be better for our family. For their part, the other elders articulated their significant unease about the ramifications such an accelerated timetable would have for the congregation. I could not help but be proud of these men. They were doing exactly what elders are supposed to do: they were watching out for the good of the flock they served and shepherded. It was such a joy to behold, and I tried to encourage them.

"Brothers, I understand where you're coming from. Though as a husband and father I am in favor of us leaving in 2017, as a pastor and fellow elder of this congregation I am with you."

In the end, our elders reached a unanimous commitment. We would be good churchmen and support the foreign mission committee's decision, even if it meant an earlier transition. But we now needed to inform the congregation as soon as possible, and they would want answers. For the former, we would call a special meeting in mid-January, as soon as the university resumed after the Christmas holidays. For the latter, we would invite James to visit our congregation a few weeks after that – not just to preach and to present on missions, but to face a congregational inquisition.

Finally, session asked me to begin preparing a new sermon series on the journeys of the apostle Paul. If our congregation was going to be facing a missions-centered pastoral transition, then we needed to hear from those portions of God's Word focused on our collective call to missions – both the call to individuals to go, and the call to churches to send.

Chapter 7:
Going Public

"It's the most wonderful time of the year..."

Spend enough time in an American retail shop in December, and you will eventually hear these words playing overhead. But for us, the Christmas and New Year season of 2016–2017 was far from wonderful. Where most family and friends meet one another with gifts, we had become the bearers of hard news. This was especially hard for me, as I have always felt tremendous anxiety at the thought of disappointing those I love and respect.

One of the first such conversations I had was with my friend "Jeremy." Jeremy is not just one of my best friends, he is also one of my oldest continuing friends – having met one another during college. We had been neighbors and coworkers at the same software firm before I went to seminary, and he was a deacon in our congregation. I highly value Jeremy's friendship, and I was afraid that this news might rupture our relationship. He and his family had relocated to our university city just a few years prior – and among their many reasons for moving was the presence of our church. We were even neighbors again! Now my family was again considering moving away. I am not an easy man with whom to be friends, but Jeremy had stuck with me through thick and thin. Yet I feared this news about China might finally prove to be a bridge too far for our friendship.

I should have known better, of course. He and his wife remain our friends to this day.

The next hard conversation was via telephone the following day with my seminary classmate, Jon. I had sent him a heads-up via email, so that he would not be blindsided. But still, it was not an easy topic to discuss. "Oh brother, I'm so sad," he said. Ever since our ministries began, we had enjoyed the opportunity to collaborate on various projects. In God's providence, there was even a direct train route from New York City to a town near the university city, and this enabled us to easily travel back and forth for in-person visits. Now all this would be finished. "But you guys will be perfect for China," he admitted.

Breaking the news to these brothers was nearly gut-wrenching. But we still had to tell our parents. This would be especially emotional, for we were not just taking away their son or daughter, but also removing five grandchildren to the far side of the world.

My wife's parents are divorced and remarried. Her mother and stepfather, along with my parents, live in the same town – and so one day I drove and met with each set of them face-to-face on my own. Her dad and stepmother lived a little further from us, and so we took the whole family to see them. While the kids were off playing in different rooms, my wife and I together shared the news with them.

If you've never had to break the heart of a person you love, then no words will suffice to describe these conversations. And if you ever have had this experience, then no words are necessary. Suffering can bring out both the best and the worst.

As the New Year holiday came and the congregational meeting approached, my wife and I also decided that it was time to inform our children. The week before the special meeting of the church, I took some special time with each of my kids to share with them that we might be moving to China. Our children were spread between the ages of twelve and four at the time, so responses varied. But the news was not easy for any of them. What about our friends? Our grandparents? Our dog? One of our kids even asked to stay behind...

The third Sunday in January arrived. Like any other Lord's Day, we went to church early for Sunday School. After Sunday School I stepped into the pulpit to lead the congregation in worship – as I had done with these same people for more than five years. We always began with announcements, and so I reminded our folks what was printed in their bulletins:

"This morning, immediately following the service, session asks those who are able, to stay for a brief, but important, informational meeting."

Shortly after this, the worship service began. Never in my life, before or since, have I had as much difficulty leading a congregation through its liturgy as I did that morning. During our responsive confession of faith from the Genevan Catechism, I distinctly remember beginning to feel a sort of vertigo. I began to wonder, "Am I actually going to be able to make it through this service?"

By God's grace, I did make it. The feeling passed, I was able to preach my sermon, and the service concluded without any more close calls. After the benediction, we asked those who could stay to be seated. The other elders came forward to sit in the front row, and I joined them there. Mercifully, session had agreed that I should not be asked to serve as spokesman on this day. A copy of two written letters was distributed to each member and adherent: a letter from session, and a letter from my wife and me. Then one of the elders entered the pulpit and began to read from the former:

"As most of you know already, session has invited James, one of the leaders of our denomination's foreign missions committee, to visit our congregation in February. What you need to know today, however, is that James is not coming merely to present to us on our church's foreign missions program. James is coming because the foreign missions committee is making a big request of us as a congregation. They have asked our pastor and his family to consider going on foreign missions service in China – and therefore they are also asking us to consider sending them..."

The letter from session concluded with an encouragement to the congregation to take some time to read the written materials, process it, and provide feedback. But we could not simply end the meeting there, so we next opened the floor for questions. Responses varied. One man was visibly angry; most were simply stunned. Some asked questions. Those we could answer, we answered. But some questions, especially related to the mission in China, were simply beyond our ken. These we encouraged our members to save for James's visit.

Over the next few days, as our people absorbed the news, questions began to trickle into my inbox. The following Sunday, therefore, we had a follow-up meeting where we provided both written and verbal responses to the most commonly asked questions. These included: "How soon will we know if the pastor is leaving?" "If they leave, how soon will they go?" "If they go, will we lose all contact with them?" "How will we find good pastoral candidates?" One dear lady, who hadn't yet quite understood that a departure for China would mean a permanent conclusion to my role as her pastor, even asked, "When are you coming back?"

"How soon will we know if the pastor is leaving?" At the time of our first announcement to the congregation, the plan was for my wife and me to take the next step – actually visiting the mission stations in China – sometime in the spring (March–May). We would then meet with the foreign missions committee for our final interview and decision in June.

But in the week between our first announcement and the follow-up meeting, there had been yet another acceleration in the process. Rob had contacted me. Rather than wait until spring to visit, he wanted us to come soon – at the beginning of February. That was only two weeks away!

This request was almost too much for our session. Here we were, trying to ease our congregation into accepting this possibility... and within two days of our first announcement, the foreign missions committee was again trying to move up the schedule! When I got off the phone with Rob, I could hardly believe it. What would the elders say to this? They had been more than patient with the process up to this point. But it seemed like every time our session adjusted, the foreign missions committee moved the goalpost.

And yet in this instance there was a significant silver lining: an earlier field visit would mean an earlier conclusion to the whole decision process. If we traveled to China at the beginning of February, we could have our final interview with the foreign missions committee at the end of February. Rather than stretch this decision over the next five months, we could have a conclusive answer in roughly thirty days. It would be a terrible scramble to execute, both for our family and for the congregation. Yet an earlier trip would bring all of us closure that much sooner – and the perceived benefits of this prevailed.

Although neither my wife nor myself regret any portion of our time in China, and though at the time we were in favor of the early trip, looking back on this period we now believe that wiser heads should have applied the brakes to this breakneck pace. Things were simply moving too fast for any of us in Pennsylvania to process matters sufficiently. One of my elders tried several times to warn me... but by this point the current was strong and swift.

Mere days before boarding our plane, we received another surprise: the foreign missions committee wanted a third change of plans. Rather than moving us directly to southwest China to work with Rob in autumn 2017, they were now proposing that we spend our first five months occupying a northeast station for a missionary due to go on furlough that year...

Chapter 8:
Meeting the Global Church

Our field visit began in the northeast. Landing at midnight, we were met at the airport by "Bruce" – the resident missionary at that station who was due for furlough. He welcomed us warmly, helped us load our belongings, and then got us underway. Bruce is one of the most energetic-for-Jesus men we have ever met. Despite the late hour, during our ride to the hotel he enthusiastically pointed out many of his city's notable features.

Having gone to bed extremely late, we had a bit of a lie-in the next morning – but not for too long. Reflecting his active personality, Bruce had a full schedule ready for us. That afternoon we were involved in an "English Corner" event, and that evening I was teaching an English-language Bible study. The next day I taught Bible study for the mission team, and on the Lord's Day I preached – with Bruce translating – in a local, unregistered church. Somewhere in the mix, we shared a meal with a local unregistered pastor.

In the Chinese context, an "unregistered church" or "unregistered pastor" is a church or pastor that has refused to register their presence and submit to the oversight of the Three-Self Patriotic Movement (TSPM) – the only officially recognized, legal Protestant body of churches in China.[1] The Three-Self Church is itself overseen by the United Front Work Department (UFWD) of the Chinese Communist Party (CCP). Because of this association with the UFWD and the CCP, many Christians and churches in China will have no involvement with the TSPM. They believe that to join the TSPM amounts to compromising the truth that Jesus – and not the CCP – is the only King and Head of the Christian Church.

Not every Chinese Christian believes this, however, and there is much evangelical ministry conducted within and through Three-Self churches. Nevertheless, all Christians acknowledge that TSPM churches are subject to periodic and varying levels of government interference with their ministry. Children under eighteen are prohibited from attending worship (thereby precluding infant baptisms), and congregations are required to display the national flag and sing the national anthem. All TSPM ordinations must be approved by the government, and only those who attend government-approved seminaries may be ordained. Enforcement varies according to region and political winds – as does obedience. For example, some TSPM churches baptized infants and taught children's Sunday School.

In between our official activities, Bruce and his wife, along with the rest of the team, did their best to show us the city and explain how life worked in northeast China. We ate a lot of good food, including dog soup – yes, dog soup. We visited the North Korean border. The highlight for both my wife and I, however, was Lord's Day worship – the first time we had ever worshiped with a congregation of Christians outside of the United States.

Our next stop was the southwest city of Chengdu – a megalopolis of over fourteen million people. Here we met more unregistered pastors, visited an unregistered seminary, and worshiped at one of two campuses of Early Rain Reformed Church. As Chengdu was to be our long-term station, we also stayed several nights in a local apartment, toured the international school, and visited the neighborhood Walmart. While Rob had flown northeast to meet us a few days prior, it

---

1.   There is one area in southeast China, Wenzhou and its surrounding counties, where Christians have special permission to gather and worship legally without joining the TSPM. This is the only exception.

was in Chengdu that we finally met his wife "Esther" and their kids.

The field visit culminated in a big interview with Bruce, Rob, and two leaders from a different organization with which Rob partnered. Over the course of about two hours, we went over a list of questions related to overseas life – the gist of which was to make sure we had as clear an idea as possible of what we were getting ourselves into. We also discussed the possibility of my family having a short-term stayover at the northeast station.

My wife was somewhat enthusiastic about the possibility of a few months in the northeast. It was a smaller city, and she had become a particular friend with one of the single ladies on the team there. I was not keen. My primary concern was the impact of uprooting our family twice over such a short period: from America to northeast China, and then from northeast to southwest China a few months later. The last-minute change of plans also felt to me like mission creep – something I had learned to be wary of in my days as an engineer.

In the end, the two leaders from the other organization supported my concerns – but they did not have a vote. The two voting members from my own denomination, Bruce and Rob, voted in favor of asking us to spend the first five months of our China ministry in the northeast. Despite my concerns, they were facing the hard reality of needing to staff the northeast station while Bruce was on furlough. They also believed that familiarization with the workings of the northeast station and experience with its local partners – the unregistered church where I had preached – would be an offsetting advantage. Though I was disappointed by this decision, my wife and I were both encouraged that Bruce and Rob believed the Lord was calling us to live and serve as part of their mission.

Our return journey was especially long, and during a ten-hour layover in a Canadian airport my wife and I had some extended time to process together what we had experienced. Our two weeks in China had confirmed our initial interest and willingness. After getting a real sense of what life was like in a major Chinese city, we both believed our family would do well in Chengdu. Both the language study and the future work appealed to us, and we seemed to mesh well with the existing team.

We also both appreciated the work in the northeast, though we were not as united on the wisdom of serving there first. We agreed, however, that we would not refuse a call on these grounds. If the foreign missions committee asked us to go to the northeast first, we would go. But I intended to be frank with the foreign missions committee regarding my outstanding concerns when we met with them for our final interview the following week.

Though our return journey was relaxed, the course of events returned to a frantic rate almost as soon as we landed back in America. Having just completed more than thirty hours of travel, we were both looking forward to a quiet drive back from Philadelphia to our home. But we had not driven more than thirty minutes out of the city when my mobile phone rang. It was James, and he was enthusiastic.

"The recommendation from the team on the field was very positive," he said, after asking about our trip. "We're looking forward to seeing you here at the main offices next week. Also," he added, "we need to get your whole family signed up for cross-cultural training as soon as possible. The training is four weeks long, in Colorado Springs. We'd like you to go in May. This program fills up quickly. Can you register in the next few days?"

I hardly knew how to reply. My wife and I were both excited about moving forward with a call to China, and given James's enthusiasm it seemed that the outcome of the coming final interview was not in serious question. Cross-cultural training was an important next step.

Nevertheless, I was still the pastor of the church in the university city. I had just been away from my people for two weeks, and had not yet even debriefed my own elders. There was no way I could unilaterally commit to leaving again for an entire month without consulting them first. "I'm going to have to talk to my session first," I reminded him.

"Of course." James understood. Prior to taking a leadership position in denominational foreign missions, he himself had been a local pastor. "Let me know. See you next week!"

The final interview with the foreign missions committee was not one interview, but three. We met with the China subcommittee, the executive committee, and finally the full committee. As expected, everybody was positive about sending us to China. As intended, I was forthright with my concerns about a stopover at the northeast station. "We aren't going to blackmail the committee," I remember saying, "if you ask us to go there, we will. But I am begging you men not to send us to the northeast."

Later that night, after returning home and tucking our children into bed, my phone rang. This time it was "Barnabas," the other full-time leader of our foreign missions committee.

"Am I talking to our next missionary to China?" he asked.

And just like that, he was. We would go to the far side of the world for our God. We would leave behind our comfortable life and happy ministry. We would give our lives to China and the future global church whose seeds were sprouting on Chinese soil and in Chinese souls. It was going to be hard – harder than we knew. But we believed Jesus was worth it. Leaving the comforts of heaven, Jesus had made the ultimate cross-cultural move for us. Facing the horrors of the cross, Jesus had embraced the ultimate personal sacrifice for us. Compared to what He had done for us, what He asked of us was minor – and He promised to go with us (Mat. 28:20). How could we say no to One who loved us so?

Before concluding, Barnabas confirmed that the committee had approved Bruce and Rob's recommendation that we begin service in the northeast. As with the military, so it is with missions: personal preferences must be subordinated, "subject to the needs of the service." This made sense, and we were not surprised, so I accepted it without further comment. Jesus works through His church, and Jesus is worth whatever He asks.

Chapter 9:
Summer of Goodbyes

The early spring of 2017 vanished in a flurry of preparations. There were numerous church meetings to prepare for the pastoral transition, both within the local congregation and in the regional presbytery. We met with a realtor about selling our home, and began the process of sifting through the accumulated possessions of fifteen years of marriage and family. What should we take with us? How much should we store long term? What things should we simply discard? It is no simple business to actually "let goods and kindred go."

By the end of April, we were ready for a break. With cross-cultural training in Colorado during May, and then another General Assembly to attend in the Midwest in early June, we decided it would be both economical and enjoyable to drive. So we piled our five children and hit the highway for the longest road trip we had ever yet undertaken as a family. On the way to Colorado Springs, we visited an old seminary classmate (and erstwhile marathon partner) of mine in western Nebraska. On the way from Colorado to General Assembly, we spent a weekend with my brother and his family in southeast Kansas.

Cross-cultural training was a substantial blessing to our family. We attended a four-week program at Mission Training International (MTI). During the first two weeks, we received a collective crash course on linguistics and language acquisition along the lines of what is commonly known as the Growing Participator Approach (GPA). For the final two weeks, our training focused on issues in cross-cultural adaptation. Most of this was classroom instruction, but we also did live exercises – including one particular high-stress simulation that left all participants somewhat floored.

Beyond the content of the training, the context of the training was itself preparatory for missionary life. We were living in close confines with men, women, and children who shared our overall heart for missions, but who came from fairly different ecclesiastical and theological traditions. This was good practice for the mission field, and we made many long-term friends. Our children still look back fondly on this period; even years later, it is not uncommon for a conversation in our home to begin, "Hey Dad, remember at MTI...?"

Our time at the General Assembly was likewise good for our family. Although this was my fourth General Assembly as a commissioner, it was our first Assembly as a missionary family – and our experience was somewhat more public. The outgoing moderator from the previous year's Assembly was an old personal friend, and he asked me to conduct and preach for the Assembly's opening worship service. When it came time for the foreign missions report, I was asked to introduce our family and our long-term hopes to come alongside Rob in "pastoring the pastors" of an emerging, slowly organizing, confessional Presbyterian denomination in China.

Besides these official moments, our family received much encouragement on the sidelines and at mealtimes. Our fourth son emerged as a social butterfly, frequently taking his meal tray and inviting himself to sit with various strangers and denominational dignitaries.

More than four thousand miles later, we returned to Pennsylvania in mid-June. I was to begin officially with the foreign missions committee the next month. However, since my congregation had "loaned" me to the committee for cross-cultural training in May, it was agreed that I would continue to serve the congregation full-time through the end of July.

A lot was happening during these last weeks in the university city. Having ended my sermon series on the journeys of Paul prior to our departure for Colorado, I spent the remaining Sundays with our congregation preaching on favorite passages submitted by our members. At home, we were busy cleaning out, packing up, and throwing away. In between all this, we were busy saying our goodbyes...

Even years later, it's hard for us to assess the separation process between our family and our congregation. Many, I think, were still grieving and simply didn't know what else to say. Nobody was in a mood to celebrate, so there was no official "going away party."

Yet despite their grief, a few families made a particular point of reaching out to us. A young couple who had hosted us in their home during our first summer serving the church made a special effort to host us again. Another couple with a little boy who shared my birthday made similar efforts to make us feel loved and cared for, even though we were breaking their hearts. One of these dear ones even had the grace to write to me once, saying that our departure to go to China was, by way of example, perhaps the greatest of many gifts we had given the church. She then added, with a digital smile, "I wondered if this would happen when you began learning Chinese. That is not a normal hobby!"

Our ministry in the university city ended on the last weekend in July. On the final Friday, the sale of our house closed and I was officially installed as an evangelist to China. Many guests attended the Friday evening installation service at our church, and one of our guest speakers was none other than Bruce – who had begun his furlough in America, and had traveled to our city expressly for the purposes of participating in my installation.

Two days later, I preached my final sermons from the university city pulpit as their pastor. In the morning, I preached my official "farewell sermon" from Psalm 139. In the evening, I concluded our ministry with a sermon from 2 Timothy 1:3-14 on "last words." At the close of that sermon, I told our congregation that Chinese people don't say "goodbye." Rather, the Chinese expression used for "goodbye" is zàijiàn – "see you again."

To say that all this was an emotional rollercoaster would be an understatement. As we wrote in a letter to our congregation, "The pain is proof that the relationships are real." Being one who hates to upset others, knowing that I was upsetting literally everybody in my life, this "summer of goodbyes" was excruciating. A friend tried to compare it to a graduation. For me it felt more like a prolonged funeral.

The month of August was a bit of a respite. Having sold our home, we lived for our last six weeks in America with my parents. My parents live in a very beautiful, rural area of south central Pennsylvania, and we spent the remainder of our days in the States soaking up the glories of trees, sunsets, and stars. We went for long walks in the woods. I took my kids to enjoy their favorite fast foods and ice cream stands. Our two oldest boys went to a foam-sword swordfighting camp. My father and uncle, both private pilots, took us for airplane rides – taking off and landing at a small airport built by my grandfather.

Last of all, less than a week before leaving the United States, my wife and daughter and I went to say goodbye to my last surviving grandmother. She was eighty-seven years old and suffering from dementia, but she remembered my wife and me – and she smiled at our daughter, who had just celebrated her fifth birthday. A little more than a year later, in October 2018 while we were living in Chengdu, Grandma went to live with Jesus forever.

September 8, 2017, the day we left for China, was the hardest day of my life. Our parents – my folks, along with my wife's mother and stepfather – accompanied us to the airport. The logistics of travel stress me, and check-in was more difficult than we anticipated. Our ticket agent decided to weigh every one of our 21 pieces of baggage – and in order to meet the weight restrictions, we had to do some last-minute shifting of carefully packed belongings.

But all of this was but minor hassle, and as nothing compared to the moment when you finally have to look your parents in the eye, give them one last hug and kiss, then say goodbye and turn away.

The men in my family do sometimes weep, but almost never in front of other people. This is not necessarily a virtue, but it is a fact. On this day we left America, both my father and I managed to hold it together. But only just.

What were we feeling that day as we boarded the flight to China and the unknown future? Here's a a verbatim copy of the entry from my journal, written through burning eyes that evening on the airplane:

> 8 September 2017
> over Nunavut, Canada
>
> Today we said goodbye to goods and kindred and boarded an airplane to China. Mum and Dad both had tears in their eyes. As we embraced, Mum simply said, "I'll miss you." Dad said, "Keep the faith." I told Mum I'd miss her, too – and to Dad I whispered, "You too." Then we went down the escalator to the security checkpoint, and they went to their cars. If home is where God wants us to be, then ALL of us are on our way home now – to different sides of the world. This is an easy thing to write, but a hard thing to do. But Jesus is worth it.

By this point, the final sentence, "Jesus is worth it," was no longer simply a theological commitment or a motto for our missionary journey. It was a visceral reality. "He left his Father's throne above," wrote Charles Wesley in a famous hymn beloved by my family. Now we had left our parents behind, too.

Chapter 10:
The Richest Man in Dongbei

Traveling to the far side of the world is a bit like time travel. We spent more than twelve hours in the air, and we also leapt forward by twelve time zones. The result was a fast-forward through time. We left America on a Friday afternoon – but did not reach our final destination in northeast China until very late Saturday night.

In English, we list the four cardinal directions on a map as "north, south, east, west." Of these four, we give priority to north and south when naming the inter-cardinal directions: we say "northeast" or "southwest," never "east-north" or "west-south." But in Chinese, the cardinal directions begin with east: *dōng-běi xī-nán* (east, north, west, south), and they give priority to east and west. Northeast China is therefore called "Dongbei" (east-north).

We were met at the Dongbei airport by a small army of new friends. Some of these were teammates who had preceded us to the field. Most of our helpers, however, were Christians from local churches with whom our team had contact. Being as tired as we were, it was a wonderful joy to find so many hands ready to assist us. Our 21 heavy bags and 5 tired children were soon divided among a small fleet of vehicles, and in less than half an hour we were moving. Arriving at our new home, our friends did not simply drop us off and wave goodbye. Despite it now being past midnight, they helped us carry everything up to our fifth floor apartment via the steps (Chinese apartment buildings are not required to have an elevator unless they exceed seven stories). Only after this did they depart.

Despite the fatigue, it was another couple of hours before we could go to bed. In order to arrange bedrooms and find pyjamas, some minimum unpacking and sorting was required. While this was ongoing, our children cautiously explored our new home – and checked the connections between the aging television in our apartment and the modern video game console they had carried so carefully across so many thousands of miles. Although it's easy for adults to criticize children regarding their interest in video games, in this case they served as a stabilizing point of familiarity amidst all that was new and foreign.

After finally getting to sleep in the wee hours, I awoke suddenly less than halfway through that first night. I had been having a nightmare – one in which my family was still trying to work our way through a Chinese airport security checkpoint. But as I lay there looking at the ceiling, a bit of light seeping into the room above the curtains, I remembered where I was and breathed a sigh of relief. The great journey was completed. We had arrived.

Our bodies, however, were not so sure – and over the next few days our family had its first experience with intercontinental jetlag. It can be quite comical. Most travelers will tell you that the best way to recover is to get yourself back on a normal sleep schedule as quickly as possible. Our first evening in Dongbei, therefore, we wanted to keep the children awake until their normal bedtime. So we tried making them play Uno, and even offering them a sugary dessert. Success was minimal. The next morning at 4:40 a.m., I again woke suddenly – but this time it was no nightmare. Rather, it was our daughter – sitting up in her bed, singing "Up from the Grave He Arose." About a half hour later, our fourth son was also awake, sitting up in his bed and looking out the window, singing "Come Thou Fount of Every Blessing." It was very sweet... but I still told them both to go back to sleep.

What was life like for our family during this first month in China? A few things stand out in our memories and correspondence. The first of these was the sheer immediacy of my work.

The Monday after our arrival, I began teaching English. There is no such thing as a "missionary visa" in China, and therefore those who desire to serve the Lord there must find a different, legally acceptable role. The Chinese are not naïve, of course; they know that many Christians come to live, study, or work in their country with ulterior motives. But for many years prior to our arrival, the general policy – at least in some regions – had been not to look too closely – so long as the authorities were not given any reason to look. Thus for the duration of our time in Dongbei, my job as an English teacher in a formal school provided the visas for our family.

Four days later, I attended my first meeting with local church leadership as part of an unregistered presbytery. Though my Chinese was light-years away from being able to conduct church business, the rest of the leadership was bilingual – and so we used English for our meetings. For the next five months I served as a "borrowed" member of this presbytery. During that time, it was interesting to note how some church issues seem universal, whereas others were definitely context-specific. As an example of the latter: on what terms can a government employee who joined the Communist Party before their conversion be received into the church? Must they explicitly renounce their Party membership, incurring official wrath, or might they allow it to expire more quietly?

The day after my first presbytery meeting, I also taught my first "underground" Bible study to local Chinese people. Technically speaking, what I was conducting was simply a free English class. Nor was this false advertising: every week, as we worked through the prepared lesson, I always took time to explain vocabulary, grammar, and idioms that were unfamiliar to my students. I enjoy words and grammar, and this was a true joy.

Yet there could also be no doubt about the true nature of this study. Classes were conducted in an apartment rather than a school, without connection to my official employment, and therefore with no legal cover should we be discovered. Moreover, I had written my curriculum based on the *Westminster Shorter*

Catechism and the English Bible. Even one of my most hardened unbelieving students referred to it as "Bible class."

Alongside this trio of new ministry labors for me, our family also spent our first month in China trying to acquire basic life logistics. Thank God we had such experienced teammates, because at the beginning we needed help with everything. What do we do for banking? How do we get SIM cards for our mobile telephones? Where do we go to buy groceries – and how do we get them all home?

This latter question is a good example of the sort of thing which is relatively simple in one's home culture, but which becomes quite a puzzle to execute in another country. A large family like ours needed a substantial amount of groceries each week. In America, therefore, my wife would simply drive to the store, fill her cart, and load the results into the boot of our minivan. But in China we had no car. What then was she to do?

My wife is a clever woman. By the end of September, she had perfected the art of feeding her hungry clan in a foreign land. This is how it worked: every Saturday afternoon, she and one of our sons would take a cab or bus to the city's big grocery store. After buying as much as they could carry, they took a different bus to a small, family-run shop closer to our home. Here they would purchase a few remaining or bulkier items: produce, juice, toilet paper, etc. The kindly shopkeeper would then agree to deliver my wife, son, and all of the groceries – even the ones purchased at the first store – right to the door of our apartment.

Groceries were not our family's only challenge. Any time our team decided to embark on an outing, we had to carefully divide up our children into smaller groups escorted by separate adults. Sometimes this was for security purposes, to avoid drawing unhelpful attention – such as when we all visited the unregistered church for a communion service on Christmas Eve. Most of the time, however, it was simply to get everybody across town via taxi.

Our family was not prepared for the level of attention we consistently garnered. Most Chinese families have one or at most two children; therefore a big family like ours became a traveling exhibition wherever we went. People loved to take pictures or videos of us – with or without our permission. Little old ladies would come up and pet our children on the head –

especially our kids with light-colored hair. None of us had ever experienced this sort of "celebrity" before.

Teaching our family to cross the street in China was another significant challenge. At first glance to a Westerner, the traffic system in Dongbei seemed based more on a dare than on any discernible order. Cabs careened through intersections, motorcycles zoomed between them, pedestrians stopped halfway across the road, and even the definition of "street" seemed fluid – wherever a vehicle could squeeze. Indeed, a few months later on my wife's birthday, she and I were honked out of the way by a car – driving on the sidewalk!

Yet for all these challenges felt by my wife and myself, it was remarkable how well our children adapted. Their adjustment had been our biggest concern prior to departing from America, yet they seemed to be handling things even better than we were. They were brave enough to taste the infamous durian fruit – a precursor of later and more exotic "adventure eating" episodes – and enjoyed going out on expeditions into the city with Mom or Dad. They usually had fun things to report during weekly Skype calls with grandparents.

In many ways, we had a typical first month – at least by missionary standards. On one hand, we experienced the "identity loss" that comes with a loss of cultural and linguistic fluency, and the language barrier was an ever-present, ever-humbling reality. On the other hand, we still possessed what matters most: our Savior, our marriage, and our kids. I was reminded of this powerfully one afternoon toward the end of the month, while I was standing in an office at school with another teacher. He asked me how many children I had, and I told him I had five. He smiled, then said quietly, "You are the richest man in Dongbei."

Chapter 11:
Sharing Jesus through Teaching English

Teaching English in a foreign culture is one of the most effective modern means of Christian witness to the world. It serves the missionary by providing income and a legitimate visa platform, and it serves the people we seek to reach by providing an attractive and useful service. The relationships forged between a caring teacher and serious students become natural bridges for discussing life's deeper issues. For the five months I taught in Dongbei, following a model Bruce had refined over many years, I saw these possibilities come alive.

At my school, significant caution was required. Less than two months after I began teaching, all of the student members of the Communist Party at my school were pulled into a meeting. They were told that every American teacher was working for the Central Intelligence Agency, and were instructed to report any teacher who mentioned religion in the classroom. Every class had an assigned "monitor" designated to take the lead in informing. A few days later I, along with every other teacher, was required to bring our passports to the school office. Upon arrival, our passports were scanned using a special app developed by the Public Security Bureau. Then we were required to look into a camera and read a sequence of numbers. It seemed clear to me that we were being voice-printed.

Because of this close scrutiny, evangelism in the classroom was more oblique than direct. Following Bruce's time-tested model, I would frequently share with my students "wise sayings" from the English language. These were verses taken from the Bible, slightly paraphrased to avoid easy sourcing via search engine.

I recast larger biblical stories and read them to my students as listening exercises. For example, the parable of the prodigal son became a story about a Scottish immigrant farmer who settled in Pennsylvania. His eldest son graduated from Harvard with a degree in agriculture and returned home to work; his younger son partied in New York City until he ran out of money and became a garbage collector. After listening to me read this story, my students had to answer questions about both its content and conclusion: from where did the farmer immigrate? Which son acted selfishly – the younger, the elder, or both? Was the farmer right to forgive his younger son, or was the elder brother correct? Was rescuing the younger son worth the cost of forgiveness?

On another occasion, I recast the biblical account of humanity's fall into a story about a young man welcomed into a magician's library. The magician invited the young man to enjoy any book in the library – with one exception. On a pedestal at the center of the library was a single book, on the cover of which was a picture of a serpent wrapped around a tree. "You must never open this book," the magician told the young man. "The magic in this book is dangerous. If you open it, you will lose your soul." But when the young man was left alone, he heard a whisper coming from the book. The voice promised to grant him three wishes if he opened the book, and told him that the magician was lying due to jealousy. So the young man opened the book, releasing a talking serpent that granted his wishes. The young man wished for unending life, money, and power. The serpent gave him immortality, a bottomless pocket of gold, and a magic word that would turn any threat to dust. The man fled the library and became wealthy and famous. But after criminals killed his wife and children while searching his home for money – which wasn't stored in the house, but came out of his pocket – the young man was overcome with anger and grief. Without thinking, he used the magic word of power – killing every living person in the world. Returning to the magician's library for help, he found the door locked. And so the story ended with him living alone in the world... forever. After reading the story, I asked my students, "How many of you would have opened the book?" Almost everybody said yes.

In addition to these in-class exercises, I also utilized interview-style speaking assignments for which I gave my students questions to prepare in advance, then met with them individually to discuss. For example, after telling them the story of the magician's library, I assigned them the following interview questions: "Imagine you were given three magical wishes. What would you wish for? Why? How do you think this wish would make you happy? How would this wish change your relationship with your family and friends?" (Despite the warning built into the story, most of my students still wished for health and riches – along with the opportunity to travel the world.) After these initial questions, I also required them to answer two final, more pointed questions: "Do you think the world would be a better place if everybody could have three magical wishes? Do you think people are basically good or basically selfish?" Though they did not think that everybody in the world should have magic wishes, most of my students still expressed the view that people were basically good. So I asked them, "Where does selfishness come from?" Many cited greed, lack of education, or poverty. But one student really surprised me when she said that she thought selfishness came from the fear of death. Still another turned the tables, "Teacher, where do you think it comes from?"

Outside of the classroom, my weekly underground Bible study was also a tremendous opportunity to share Jesus through teaching English. Here there was no need to be oblique, for there was a tacit understanding among my students that the "price" of free English lessons was a curriculum based on the Bible. Further, I told my students that I could not force them to believe and would not try; only God can change the heart. My goal was for them to understand the message clearly. On this foundation, our class proceeded with honesty and mutual respect.

In the first week's class, we discussed the "chief aim" of human life. I emphasized to my students that whether or not a person is part of an official religion, everybody has a goal for which they must make sacrifices, and each of us has a plan that we follow to reach our goals. These goals that we serve are our gods. The plans that we follow are our Bibles. One member of the class readily agreed, telling us all quite honestly, "English is my god." He then told us how he had made personal sacrifices to pursue it. Odd as it may sound, this was an encouraging admission: for though it was obvious that his heart was unchanged, it was also evident that the day's teaching had not been unclear.

As the "semester" unfolded, we progressed through the biblical teaching summarized in the *Shorter Catechism* (using a modernized English version), following up each summary by reading and discussing a supporting passage of Scripture. We discussed the fall of humanity and original sin using the analogy of a sports team. Just as a team captain can make good or bad decisions that affect the whole team, so humanity's first team captain, Adam, made a terrible decision that ruined all of his ordinary descendants. After discussing the word "ordinary," we also discussed the word "extraordinary" – and how God did the extraordinary thing of starting a new team with a new Captain. Subsequent lessons included explorations of Jesus' teachings on His own identity, the meaning of His death – we had a great discussion of the word "atonement" – and the historicity of His resurrection.

Rarely have I ever felt more fulfilled as a pastor and teacher than I did in these times of walking unbelievers through the foundations of the gospel – and all via the medium of teaching them a second language. There was something exceptionally special about serving outward and inward needs simultaneously. It was challenging, definitely. But I loved it.

Before we left Dongbei, the Saturday morning class had covered a wide range of gospel topics – and in one case led to some very interesting follow-up. "Rick" had been a student of the Saturday morning studies long before I ever landed in China. Over the course of my time in his city, he became more than just a student – he became a friend. He occasionally gave me rides after class, gave me a tour of his workplace, and organized an impromptu celebration for my birthday. During our last month in Dongbei, he took the rare step of inviting me to his home for one-on-one Bible study. We met like this several times, and in our last meeting he confessed to me that he had known for several months that the Bible has power – which is why he had been avoiding reading it! At the farewell dinner he organized with my Saturday students for our family, he stood up and said that our work had "affected" them and made them want to learn the Bible. May the Lord save him yet.

Beyond the opportunities and the pleasures that arose from the study itself, my weekly Saturday morning trek to the meeting place played a formative role in our development as missionaries. Like nothing else in all of our experience, either preceding or subsequent, it forced me regularly to face the unsettling question: *what if today is the day you are caught?*

My previous experience of open-air evangelism in Pennsylvania had taught me that one could never permanently vanquish fear in this life: I felt it every time I prepared to speak on the campus in that university city. Week after week, even semester after semester, I always felt it gnawing at me. The experience had taught me that courage was not the absence of fear; courage was doing what was right despite the presence of fear.

I found the same to be true in Dongbei. Every week as I walked alone through the city to teach my underground study, the same questions would hiss in my heart: *what if today is the day the police knock on the door? There won't be any way to hide what you're doing... what will happen then? What might they do to your family?*

This is how fear works – by casting our imaginations into unknown realms of terrifying hypotheticals. But as the weeks passed, the Lord sustained me. Early on the morning of my birthday, near the end of our stay in Dongbei – one of my last Saturdays teaching the illegal study – I wrote these words in my journal: "Fear allows circumstances to overshadow Christ's promises, but faith interprets circumstances in the light of Christ's promises."

Chapter 12:
What Is a Life?

By the time China's "National Day" arrived at the beginning of October, we had been on the field for almost a month. "National Day" (*Guóqìngjié*) commemorates 1 October, 1949 – the day on which Mao Zedong stood atop the Tiananmen Gate of the Forbidden City in Beijing and proclaimed the beginning of the People's Republic. The National Day itself is the beginning of one of China's annual "Golden Weeks" (*Huángjīnzhōu*) – a week-long holiday period during which schools close and many families travel. National Day is essentially the Chinese equivalent of the Fourth of July – except that it lasts for an entire week.

Around this same time annually, though it varies due to fluctuations in the lunar calendar, the Chinese celebrate a much more ancient holiday, the Mid-Autumn Festival (*Zhōngqiūjié*). Mooncakes are a traditional food associated with this holiday, and we received several packages of these as gifts from Chinese friends. The cakes come with various fillings – eggs, nuts, beans, etc. – and we found them for sale everywhere in our city.

Just before my students went home for the holiday, I gave my first exam. For the speaking portion of this test, I asked my students to answer one of the following questions: 1) If you only had 24 hours to live, what would you do? 2) If you could change one thing about the world, what would you change? 3) If you could change one thing about yourself, what would you change? All three are variations on a more fundamental question: what is a life?

As the excitement of our early weeks passed into the patterns of daily and weekly routine, as the foreign gradually transformed into the familiar, our whole family began to feel the distance and loss of people and places left behind in America. This sense of loss was compounded by the good news from home that our former congregation in Pennsylvania was moving forward with a candidate to succeed me as their pastor. In mid-October, my wife wrote the following in a letter to a friend:

> As always, it is so good to hear from you. I am sorry I never got a chance to reply to last week's email. Honestly, when I read it, I had a bit of an emotional time... It made me think of you all and, although I am very happy and pleased that things are moving forward with [the new pastoral candidate and his wife], it was just an emotional moment for me thinking of how they are taking our place in a sense. And of course it made me think of our church family and all of you and it made me miss everyone...

Striking a similar tone, I wrote the following to a different friend about a month later:

> This may sound weird, but I sometimes think about where my wife and I will end up when our work is finished and all of our kids are grown and gone. There's really no way to know, of course – but I sometimes imagine a small little ranch house, maybe about the size of a cabin. Maybe we will be so urbanized by that point that we'll end up in a city – but there's still a lot of the Shire in our hearts, so maybe it will be the country after all. I miss rural Pennsylvania often: sunlight filtering down through a forest canopy, or walking along leaf-strewn paths in the fall, are some of the enduring images in my life.

Though our kids also missed family and friends in Pennsylvania, the great fundamentals of their life were essentially the same. Because they had been homeschooled from the beginning, their greatest playmates had always been one another. That was still the case in China. They were still able to play games together, and spoke to their grandparents at least weekly. We were also very intentional about ensuring that each child continued to receive their weekly "special time" with Dad.

"Special time" was a practice that our family had instituted while we still lived in America, but which became exponentially more important once we moved to China. It works like this: each of our five children is assigned a weekday (Monday – Friday) on which they get special one-on-one time with Dad in the evening apart from the rest of their siblings. Sometimes this "special time" was spent reading a book. Other times we watched funny videos online. We might go for a walk and buy small snacks, or sometimes we would go out for a meal – which was significantly more affordable in China than in America. What we did on any given occasion was not so important; what was important was that we were consistent and intentional about doing something together. Humanly speaking, I think that this system of "special time" was one of the most important factors in sustaining our children through our cross-cultural transition.

For my wife and I, however, the experience was more complex. Though we still had our children and each other, so much else about our lives had changed. My wife's role remained that of wife, mother, and home educator – yet even the most basic tasks associated with that role, such as grocery shopping, were exponentially more challenging. Every time she left the home she was faced with the intimidation of the language barrier, and she felt it deeply. Likewise, I too was feeling a profound sense of identity loss. In my own language, I was used to being an accomplished communicator: my pastoral vocation involved public speaking, and I was a published author. But in China I could barely manage the most basic conversational exchange – and my workload as an English teacher allowed very little time to study Chinese.

There was a theological lesson in all of this, of course. If our Lord Himself laid aside His glory and took the form of a servant to rescue us, should we not be willing to surrender our own "glory" in following and serving Him? We did not have any doubt about the answer to this question. But what was sweet as a theory proved bruising as a reality, and we hurt. In mid-December, I wrote the following in an extended letter to one of our closest friends:

I have been reading to our third son from *The Fellowship of the Ring*. Tonight we finished "The Council of Elrond." At the end of that chapter is when Frodo realizes that his journey doesn't stop at Rivendell. He will have to take the Ring to Mordor. Tolkien describes it thus:

> A great dread fell on him, as if he was awaiting the pronouncement of some doom that he had long foreseen and vainly hoped might after all never be spoken. An overwhelming longing to rest and remain at peace by Bilbo's side in Rivendell filled all his heart. At last with an effort he spoke, and wondered to hear his own words, as if some other will was using his small voice. "I will take the Ring," he said, "though I do not know the way."[1]

I cannot tell you the number of times I have felt like Frodo in this last year. I often dream about retirement in some quiet "Rivendell." Sometimes I even daydream about scenarios that would allow us to return honorably to our former life of comfort in the "Shire." It's not because I don't want to do the work before us. Nor is it because I have ceased to believe that Jesus is worth whatever He asks. It's simply because I feel dislocated from the people and places I value, and that dislocation stings...

Although we are further away from our former life, you are further along the path of life's expectations and disappointments. So I think what I am learning can also be a lesson for you, dear sister. God has a way of disrupting our finely laid plans and dearly cherished assumptions about what our lives should look like. Many times when we were contemplating leaving Pennsylvania – and many times since – I have come back to a simple question, "What is a life?" Put another way – what is life supposed to be about? I already know the answer... "What is the chief aim of man?"

I've taken a long road to make a simple point: we need to be careful about Norman Rockwell. At its best, his work is a reminder that we were made for a better world. At its worst, it is snare to make us think we should expect

---

1.   J.R.R. Tolkien, *The Lord of the Rings* (Boston: Houghton Mifflin, 1987), 284.

that world now. I've come to that conclusion about my own Frodo-maginations. At their best, they are a homesickness for a better world and may be embraced. But if they are allowed to replant wrong assumptions about what I should expect in this world, then they must be cast into the fires of Mount Doom.

The many things that both of you are doing are brushstrokes in something much better than a Norman Rockwell painting. The disruption of your expectations of normalcy is part of the beautiful mess of a God who chooses to use men and women rather than angels. To quote Tolkien's friend [C.S. Lewis, *The Last Battle*], God is using you to help fill in the pages of "the Great Story which no one on earth has read: which goes on forever: in which every chapter is better than the one before."[2]

Jesus said, "No one who puts his hand to the plow and looks back is fit for the kingdom of God," (Luke 9:62). Throughout our time in China, but especially in those early months, homesickness was not infrequent – nor was it easy to differentiate between true heavenly longing and simple earthly desires. The only answer was the question, "What is a life?"

---

2.   C.S. Lewis, *The Last Battle* (New York: Collier, 1981), 184.

Chapter 13:
Why Missionaries Send So Many Pictures of Food

Apart from the prayers of God's people in America, the most important factor in our family's adjustment were people. Some of these were voices of encouragement from afar: a dear older sister in Christ from our former church in Pennsylvania wrote to us several times each month, and my friend Jon made it a point to call me every week. I was the only male member of our team while we served in Dongbei, and having another guy to talk to during those first five months was a sustaining spiritual boost.

Even closer to "home," however, were the three single ladies who served with us on the field. Each of them had substantial experience in China, and all of them went out of their way to help us whenever we needed assistance. They helped me come up to speed quickly with teaching English, and they helped my wife find the best groceries. They would help order takeouts for our team meetings, and they loved our children. One of them took my wife to Chinese Bible studies at the unregistered church, and another tutored us in Chinese. They did all of these things while at the same time carrying their own substantial loads of teaching, one-on-one meetings, and other missionary labors. These three sisters were, in every sense of the word, a God-send. We would not have survived without them.

One of the first photos I have is of our family sitting in a restaurant with two of these ladies, less than a week after our arrival. It's funny, because later one of them said to us, "I feel like the only pictures I ever send home are pictures of food." But there is a good reason for this.

Gospel ministry in closed countries like China is extraordinarily sensitive, and the "normal" level of caution required is generally far beyond what most Americans can imagine. But Chinese people love to go out for tea or for a meal, and Chinese restaurants are generally far more affordable than their American equivalents. Indeed, it is more common for a Chinese friend to invite you to dinner in a restaurant than in their own home. For these reasons, meeting local friends at a restaurant is often a great way to minister to them. It's generally safe, it's typically cheap, and it flows "with the grain" of Chinese culture.

Dining at Chinese restaurants, however, also means being willing to branch out in terms of cuisine. Sometimes this was a pleasure, as when we were introduced to *yángròu chuànr* – lamb kabobs that you roast right at your table and then dip in various spices. Both my wife and I also developed a taste for sweet potato lattes. Although they sound strange, and their purple color bore an unsettling resemblance to stomach medicine, the taste was fairly amazing – significantly better than the pumpkin spice lattes that are the annual autumn obsession in America.

In mid-November, our friend James came to visit on behalf of the denomination's foreign missions committee. Part of his visit involved the two of us going out for supper with a local unregistered pastor. This proved to be my introduction to two new local specialties...

At my suggestion, the local pastor, "Seth," made a reservation for us to eat *yángròu chuànr*. Alongside this main course, Seth also ordered some roasted pig heart. I thought this might be a stretch, but I trusted Seth and would at least give it a try. Then James spoke up.

"Let's order some silkworm larvae!"

Obliging his guest, Seth placed the order for several skewers' worth of silkworm larvae. When the food arrived, there they were: twelve dark, bulbous pupae, skewered and waiting for us to roast alongside our *chuànr*. But there was one noteable difference...

The silkworm pupae were still wiggling.

I'm not joking. Apparently, it is standard practice for the pupae to be served alive – so that we could roast them for ourselves over the coals on our table. Once they stopped moving and began to ooze... then, Seth instructed me, they would be ready to eat.

I ate one silkworm pupa out of curiosity, then a second – simply to prove to myself that I had the courage. After that, I was finished with this new flavor. Silkworm larvae taste better than green peas, but only just. Seth, who was sitting beside me, only ate one. Noticing this at some point, I turned to him.

"Do you like these?" I asked.

He simply shook his head. After that, the two of us gladly left the remaining dozen pupae to James. In my judgment, he deserved every bite.

The roasted pig heart was a much more pleasant surprise. It came out pre-cooked, and had a taste like bacon. Seth told me that it pairs particularly well with red wine – though on that evening, we only had cola to drink.

Less than a week later, we were able to turn the tables – in a more familiar direction – when we invited Seth, his family, and several other Chinese friends to Thanksgiving dinner with our team. It was the first any of them had celebrated American Thanksgiving. My wife had not been able to find any turkey in the stores, so she made some spice-rubbed chicken – which turned out to be even more delicious. With supplies sent from America, she was also able to prepare a pumpkin pie. The Chinese have a word for pumpkin – *nánguā* ("south melon") – but none of our friends had ever before tried eating *nánguā* pie. It was a real pleasure to be able to serve them this very traditional American dessert.

One of the greatest privileges of my time in Dongbei was getting to serve alongside Seth in the local unregistered presbytery. Personally mentored for many years by my colleague Bruce, Seth is a devoted servant of Jesus Christ: hard-working and long-suffering, with a sharp mind and a pastor's heart. He will probably never be famous in this life, but he is one of those men whose dedication and tireless efforts put my own to shame. During my time in Dongbei, he invited me once to preach for his congregation. My spoken Chinese being still in its infantile stages, he himself had to translate – and well do I remember catching a glimpse of his well-marked, pre-written translation of my sermon. I had hoped that by agreeing to preach, I was giving this brother a bit of a break. But from the look of things, he had put in quite a bit of preparation.

Security considerations forbid me from saying much more about Seth, his ministry, or his family. But as I reflect upon the people who encouraged us and introduced us to exotic cuisine, I will share just two more memories involving him...

Once, after the conclusion of a meeting of the unregistered presbytery, I invited Seth to go to lunch. He agreed, and led me to a restaurant tucked back within a residential area. When he asked what I wanted to order, I asked him to order some of his favorites. One of these was a fish dish that came out whole, including the eyes. I was told once that Chinese people like to see the whole fish (rather than just the meat) on the plate, because it guarantees that what you are served is exactly what you ordered – a smart move in any culture.

Yet what I remember most from my meal with Seth is not what we ate, but rather what he said at one point. We were discussing the general contours of Christian ministry, when at one point he said, with a bit of a sigh, "Being a pastor is hard." In that moment I really resonated with him – more than I had expected. For as isolated as I had felt, here at last was another man with whom I shared a true connection. Humanly speaking, we were from opposites sides of the world. Yet spiritually we shared a double bond: as brothers in Christ, and as colleagues in ministry.

The last memory I will share of Seth involves a final food recommendation he gave me. As we neared the end of our time in Dongbei in late January 2018, my two eldest sons came to me with a surprising request:

"Dad, will you take us to a dog restaurant?"

Though very uncomfortable to Americans, gǒuròu ("dog meat") is a perfectly acceptable alternative to more traditional meats – and there are special "cattle" dogs. Although dog meat is not as widely consumed as is sometimes reported, it is considered a delicacy in some parts of China. My wife and I had tried it on our exploratory trip to China a year earlier. Now I was more than willing to allow my sons the same experience. What a sign of their desire to enter our host culture! But where to take them, and what to order?

It did not take me long to seek Seth's counsel – and his advice proved expert like only local knowledge can. He informed me precisely where to go, and told me exactly which dishes to order: a dog meat hot pot, and a side of dog ribs. Both were good, but the latter was the most delicious. All three of us agreed that dog tastes a lot like turkey – dark meat turkey. If only we had known in time for Thanksgiving.

"It makes me happy to know that dogs taste good," said my second son as we were leaving the *gǒuròu guǎn* ("dog meat restaurant") that night.

I nodded. "Man's best friend, in life or in death." I sent a picture with our next weekly letter.

Chapter 14:
Christmas Adam

It was a Saturday morning in December, exactly three months after we had landed in China. That morning, I discussed with my underground Bible study the historicity of the resurrection of Jesus. We read portions from Matthew, Luke, John, and 1 Corinthians 15. When we got to the place where the apostle Paul writes about more than five hundred people seeing Jesus alive at the same time, one lady, who had not yet made a clear confession of faith, said, "So it must be true!"

Later that morning, as I sat in my favorite coffee shop overlooking our city and writing emails, my wife sent me the contact card for a local bakery using WeChat, the ubiquitous Chinese social media app. Connecting to the bakery via this same app, I placed an order – without using any English. In the moment, it was a very modest task. Yet not long after hitting "send" on the order, the realization struck me: we had just ordered groceries via WeChat using only Chinese!

Both my wife and I were making progress in Chinese. We had two tutors coming to our apartment weekly, and by the end of the semester their labors were bearing fruit: we could both recite from memory the Apostles' Creed in Chinese. *"Mànman lái,"* the Chinese like to say. This translates literally to something like, "Slowly slowy it comes." Slowly indeed... but our Chinese was coming.

On the other hand, our time in Dongbei was also coming towards its conclusion. My colleague Bruce would be returning at the end of January, and we were living in his apartment. Before he landed, we would need to be on an airplane to our next station...

On my final day as a classroom teacher, I gave my students a special surprise: my whole family, along with our teammates and another friend, came to class and sang English Christmas carols to them. The size of our family never failed to impress, and the singing touched many hearts. As one student wrote on her course evaluation form, "I saw the lovely five children and they gave us a song. I felt happiness at that time."

After the music faded, I gave my students their final lesson. It was a listening exercise, and the content was a cultural lesson about how different global cultures celebrate Christmas. We talked about how people observe the holiday in Finland, Germany, the UK, the USA, Japan, Bolivia, and Venezuela. Most people in China see Christmas as a Western holiday. My goal was to show them that Christmas is a global holiday.

As part of this lesson, I also explained to them the origin of the holiday's name by telling them a bit about the extraordinary birth of Jesus. In so doing, I laid special emphasis on the fact that the first people to celebrate Christmas were not wealthy Westerners, but rather poor Middle Eastern shepherds. Likewise, the first Christmas gifts ever given came not from Westerners, but from scholars from the East. Christmas was never intended to be a Western holiday. From the beginning, it was meant as a celebration for the whole world.

On 17 December, I conducted my first international baptism. "Alex" had professed faith privately before Bruce went on furlough. The privilege of baptizing him fell to me. As I recorded in my journal, "Today was the happiest day of the semester."

On 23 December, my sons announced to me that it was "Christmas Adam" – since it was the day before Christmas Eve, and Adam was created before Eve. That same morning, our whole team threw a Christmas party for the people from my Saturday morning underground Bible study. We sang songs, ate cookies, and gave gifts. Most of our Chinese friends had never before received a Christmas present.

We ended the party with an explanation of how the joy of Christmas becomes our personal joy. God's grace and peace are gifts to all who desire them, but they only become ours if we receive and rest upon Jesus. To demonstrate, I pointed to a chair and said, "*Ēnhuì. Píng'ān.*" ("Grace. Peace.") I picked up the chair, sat it down, then sat upon it. "*Xìn.*" ("Faith.")

On Christmas Eve, our entire family attended worship at Seth's unregistered church. To get there without attracting too much attention, we divided our children into three groups, and two of our teammates each took a pair of kids with them – leaving at slightly offset times. Last of all, my wife and I followed with our daughter. In God's goodness, all went well. Most of the service was conducted in Chinese, and therefore difficult for us to understand. But when it came to the Lord's Supper, the bread and the wine speak a language of their own: we knew what was being said, even though we did not know the words. Sharing the Lord's Supper is perhaps the most beautiful way possible in this world to experience the truly cross-cultural nature of the church.

Two days before the New Year, I was again in my favorite coffee shop overlooking our city. As I sat there writing, the janitor stopped at my table. She picked up my hat, which had fallen on the floor, and handed it back to me. "*Xièxiè,*" I said. ("Thank you.")

Her reply was surprising: "*Yēsū ài nǐ.*" ("Jesus loves you.")

I was so touched, it took me a moment before I could reply in turn, "*Yēsū yě ài nǐ.*" ("Jesus also loves you.") As we looked toward the end of our time in Dongbei and yet another major transition, these words from an anonymous sister were a powerful reminder that God's love is always closer than we imagine.

Our final weeks in Dongbei were fast and full. Though my classroom responsibilities had concluded, numerous team evangelistic activities were ongoing – all while our family was packing for the move to southwest China. Of our original 21 suitcases, we planned to ship 14 of them ahead of us. So my wife was busy sorting between essential and non-essential items – and I was scrambling to finish my final Bible studies.

On the last Saturday morning with them, I spent some time reviewing with the members of my underground class. I laid special emphasis on the idea of accountability and responsibility. In any subject, students are accountable for what they are taught. Just so, I told my students: they would be accountable to God for what they had learned from me. They need to decide what they believe. But how could they do this?

I suggested to my students that one of the best ways to clarify and evaluate their beliefs would be to actually write out their personal answers to the big questions of life: where did the world come from? Why were people, including them and me, so selfish? What would happen to them when they die? Where can they find hope?

My point on this last Saturday with them was strikingly similar to the one I had made in our first time together: whether we are serious about religion or not, our answers to these questions constitute our own personal "confessions of faith." To give them an example, I took my students through my own personal summary of the gospel – which I had written before leaving Pennsylvania. I ended with a reminder and an encouragement: although that morning might be the last time I would see any of them in this world, my sincere desire was to see all of them again in heaven.

On that last day, one of our most hardened skeptics – the man who began the semester confessing, "English is my god" – surprised me by asking the first spiritual question he'd ever voiced in my presence: "Are Christians happier than people without religion?"

Quite honestly, I told him that the answer was complicated. Sometimes people who don't think about God and who are comfortable enough to avoid suffering are quite happy – at least for a season. And sometimes Christians have to do things for God that make them very sad or afraid – like moving to the other side of the world. But in the end, the big question is not whether we are happy. The question is whether we have hope. Are we ready to meet God when we die? Christians have a strong, sure hope that God will accept us – not because we are good, but because Jesus was good for us.

After class, I took my third son – who had accompanied me that day – to my favorite coffee shop. As we sat together looking out the windows at the city, he told me how he missed his grandparents. I told him I missed them, too – and for a few moments after that, neither one of us spoke. Our time in Dongbei had been good. But it had not been without cost.

Amidst the bustle of our final preparations to depart, I was struck by the handful of loose ends we would leave behind us in Dongbei. My one-on-one studies in Rick's home had barely begun. What would become of his new openness? Would it continue after Bruce returned, or would Rick retreat once more into his former pretense of agnosticism? I also wondered about the friendships we had developed with our Dongbei teammates who weren't moving with us. Would those friendships continue? How would our sisters' stories grow and change as we went our separate ways?

Yet in reality, there is no such thing as a loose end. If it ever seems otherwise, it is simply because our eyes cannot yet behold the hand that hung the stars – the hand that currently holds and upholds all things, including every thread of the human story. As we finished our days in northeast China, I reminded myself that God's work was bigger than any of us. As we closed one chapter and opened another, this was both humbling and reassuring.

Our journal entries from January 2018 show hearts of hope and thankfulness. About two weeks before we left Dongbei, my wife wrote the following:

> Our adventure has only begun! We are closing perhaps the first chapter of this adventure as we prepare to leave Dongbei, but I think we are all excited about what the Lord has in store for us as we embark on the next chapter in Chengdu. What an honor and privilege it is to be His daughter, to serve my family, to learn another language for His glory, to meet brothers and sisters in our newly adopted country and also meet those who don't know Him, but are eager to learn more. I hope I can play some small part – even if it is something as simple as a smile – showing Christ's love in me towards those I meet. Praise the Lord for His kingdom around the world!

The Lord's goodness and faithfulness filled our hearts. He had brought us safely around the world and successfully through our first phase of missionary life. My last journal entry for January, written the morning after we landed in Chengdu, echoed my wife's buoyant spirit:

> A road that began with a prayer in June 2015 and a phone call in October 2016 came to its first waypoint late last night as we arrived in Chengdu, having completed four and a half months in Dongbei. God be praised for the road traveled; God be merciful for the road ahead.

Chapter 15:
Teahouses, Truth, and Talking Pandas

There is an old proverb about Sichuan province in southwest China: if you go there, you will see more teahouses than sunny days. This testimony is true.

Chengdu, the capital of Sichuan, has more than fourteen million people. It is built in a geological basin at the eastern end of the Chinese Himalayas, which prevents most of the city smog from rising high enough to dissipate – leaving the urban sprawl almost constantly overcast. Only rarely would one see blue skies in Chengdu. Otherwise, we lived under the undifferentiated, unpunctuated grey blanket referred to in our family as the "uni-cloud."

Yet despite this grumpiness overhead, Chengdu is a very warm place. As to climate, it is in a subtropical latitude, which makes for mild winters and humid summers. As to culture, the locals will frequently tell you: "Chengdu is a very relaxed city." The feel of Chengdu is very *suíbiàn* ("as you please" or "casual"), and the city is said to have ten thousand teahouses. These are some of the most colorful, vivacious places I have ever experienced.

In fact, my favorite spot in all of China was a riverside teahouse just a few blocks from our apartment. For the equivalent of less than a dollar, I could enjoy a bottomless mug of healthy green tea, study Chinese or smoke my pipe, and enjoy the sights and sounds of hundreds of Chinese retirees playing *wéiqí* (a game of black and white stones), *xiàngqí* (Chinese chess), or *mahjong* – all the while drinking tea, smoking cigarettes, and conversing boisterously. Not long after we arrived in Chengdu, a friend from Pennsylvania wrote to me, "Joy is a conscious decision to live life in the knowledge that God is good and has good plans for us." But more than once I was convicted by what I observed at the riverside teahouses: how is it that these, my Chinese neighbors, most of whom had no hope of life beyond death, seemed so full of the simple joy of living – indeed, so much fuller than I?

Outside of China, Chengdu is most famous as the home of the Giant Panda Base – the world's premier research facility for the breeding, rearing, and study of panda bears. Giant pandas appear everywhere in the city's iconography. In some of the older taxis, you could even hear an automated message in both Chinese and English when your ride began: "Welcome to Chengdu, home of giant pandas and beautiful lanterns."

Our welcome to Chengdu came at the tail end of January 2018. We were joining a large team, and many of them met us at the airport. As with our first arrival in Dongbei, our baggage and children were promptly divided between multiple conveyances, and we were all swiftly whisked away to our new home between the city's first and second ring roads. By Chinese standards, our apartment was spacious – with large windows to soak up the natural light. It had been cleaned, furnished, and filled with warm touches: a welcoming banner, essential groceries for a few meals, and a freshly baked batch of cinnamon rolls. Rob and Esther lived in the same building, and so the morning after our arrival their children joined ours for some lively rounds of Mario Kart. It was a good start.

An important task for our first week in Chengdu was applying for new visas. Because I was changing roles from teaching English to studying Chinese, and since my family's visas were all attached to mine, all seven of us had to apply for brand new residence permits. Prior to our arrival in Chengdu, there had been a significant amount of uncertainty surrounding this moment. Nobody expected our applications to be rejected, but there was a real question about whether one or more of us would have to leave the country in order to process the change in status. Different inquiries had yielded different responses.

It was therefore with some uncertainty that Esther escorted our family to the visa office at the heart of Chengdu. As a native Chinese speaker with a particular gift for persuading others to be helpful, Esther enabled us to navigate the reapplication process with fluency – and without the *máfan* ("hassle") of having to leave the country. However, when I sat down with the visa officer for my personal interview, I was not quite prepared for some of the questions I received.

"Why did you break your contract to teach English in Dongbei? Your contract was for a year, but you left after only one semester."

Answering official questions in a culture closed to foreign missionaries is a tricky business. As a Christian, outright lying is not an option. As a missionary, the whole truth is also not prudent. Jesus said, "Behold, I am sending you out as sheep in the midst of wolves, so be wise as serpents and innocent as doves," (Matt. 10:16). The challenge is to say only true things – but not the whole truth.

In answer to this first question, therefore, I did not explain that it had always been the plan of our mission to relocate my family after one semester. Rather, I told her something else that was true: "It is too difficult to teach English and study Chinese at the same time."

"Why did you move to Chengdu? Why not just stay and study Chinese in Dongbei?"

This question was more incisive than it appears. Every Chinese person knows that Dongbei is a much better place to study Mandarin than Chengdu. The reason for this is simple: standard Mandarin, *Pǔtōnghuà* (the "common speech") comes from the Dongbei region of China. By contrast, many people in Chengdu grow up speaking *Sìchuānhuà* ("Sichuanese") – an almost entirely different language. Even when Sichuan people speak *Pǔtōnghuà*, their accent is heavy and difficult to understand. For ease of learning Mandarin, it would have made much more sense to remain in the region of Dongbei.

Again, I spoke true things – but not the whole truth. "I have a friend who lives here in Chengdu. He recommended the university here."

The most difficult question came last. "You have a big family, and you are going to be a full-time student. Where do you get your money?"

Now what? Obviously it would be unwise to confess that I received a salary as a foreign missionary. To do that would not only have meant deportation for us; it might well have endangered other teammates such as Rob and Esther. But what could I say that was true?

"Before I came to China, I saved money..." This was true. Though our capacity for savings dropped dramatically after our children began arriving, and especially after I left engineering for full-time ministry, we had always been intentional about savings.

"We also have investments..." This was also true. I had retirement funds rolled over from my engineering days, as well as funds contributed during our years in pastoral ministry. My wife also had some mutual funds. We weren't drawing on these, but theoretically we could.

"We had a house in America that we sold..." Also true. Again, we were not actively drawing on the proceeds from the sale of our house – but in theory we could.

"Our family gives us money." This was the thinnest ice. Of course our parents did occasionally send us money, but in reality here I was using "family" to refer not to our biological family, but rather to our church family. In the weekly letters I wrote as a missionary, I always referred to the church as "the Family."

Thankfully, the officer did not press the point – and with these answers she seemed satisfied. She required me to write it all down for her on a piece of paper and sign my name, then she put the signed statement with our other papers. We were given receipts, and told we would be notified when our visas were ready.

The next day – only our fourth day in Chengdu – we took our children and a Dongbei teammate who had traveled with us to the Giant Panda Base. It was a delightful adventure for our whole clan – especially for our youngest son, who often enjoyed pretending that he was an imaginary talking animal called "Baby Panda." Now, for the first time in his life, he saw real-life baby pandas with their parents – along with red pandas and roaming peacocks. We made lots of good memories so crucial in the early days of a new place, snapped some excellent photos, and the kids all came home with souvenirs.

A special memory from this trip concerns my daughter, who was five years and purchased a plush panda doll. Going with a feminized version of the word "Oreo," she decided to name her bear "Orea." As we were riding the subway on the way home, I tried to make Orea talk...

"Dad, she isn't real yet – because she still has her tag on." My mistake...

Despite this glaring error, and despite the tense questions of the day prior, our arrival in Chengdu felt very smooth. It was the middle of winter, but we were living in a bright apartment among good company in a mild climate. The accent buzzing in our ears was daunting, but soon we would begin studying the language in earnest. We were living in a megalopolis – Chengdu has more people than the entire state of Pennsylvania! – but we were part of a well-established, settled team. It all seemed very *suíbiàn*, just as the local motto said: "Chengdu is a very relaxed city."

Chapter 16:
Some Time to Exhale

Roughly two weeks after landing in Chengdu, I wrote the following in a letter to a couple from our former church in Pennsylvania:

> Our arrival in Dongbei was heavy and hurried: we had the weight of so many goodbyes, the hassle of so many logistics, and then almost no time to settle in before I had to leap into work (landing late Saturday, teaching Monday). By contrast, our transition to Chengdu has been much less stressful: we shipped baggage in advance, our friends here had a lot of things ready for us, and we have been enjoying several weeks to settle in before language classes start...
>
> In the meantime, we have some time to exhale. In a way, it's the first time since October 2016 (when this transition all began) that we've had any time like this. There's no packing to do, no move to plan, no stress of looming goodbyes, and no waves of unfamiliar tasks careening toward us... just a few weeks to settle, and then begin learning a new language. For once, it seems we are not in frantic motion. That's been nice: we've been able to sleep in a bit, take our kids sightseeing, catch up

on reading, watch a few movies, pray every morning...
and yesterday, for the first time in years, my wife and
I actually went out on Valentine's Day. (We went to a
Tibetan-influenced Indian restaurant, where they serve
Yak meat curry!)

Three days later, my wife wrote the following in her journal:

Here we are in Chengdu! Sometimes I pause and think
about that... Wow! I remember this feeling and keen
interest I had in this city before we even thought about
coming to China at all. I think it is the Lord's way to put
certain things, places, and people on your mind. I am
happy to be here and serve, and I hope I can be useful,
at least in some small way, to our team here.

These paragraphs give a good summary of the real sense of
relief that settled over us as we began to settle into life in
Chengdu. More than three years of transition had finally come
to fruition. At last we were in a place where we could expect
to remain indefinitely – and we could walk to Walmart from
our side gate. Perhaps it would be going too far to say that our
life was "normal," but at least it was acquiring a manageable
regularity.

The linchpin of any serious Christian life is Lord's Day worship
and the fellowship it fosters with other believers. Church had
always been the center of our family's life, Sunday worship the
central axis around which everything else orbited. In America
this was a relatively straightforward affair: we simply drove to
the public facility where the church gathered. In China, things
were a bit more complicated.

Our first Sunday morning came less than a week after
we landed in Chengdu. Where would we worship? Practices
among our teammates varied. Some attended Chinese Church
in one of the unregistered Presbyterian congregations. Some
occasionally visited the International Fellowship – a legally
permitted, interdenominational congregation for expatriates
that met in the basement of the city's largest Three-Self (TSPM)
church facility. Still others on our team had joined a home-
based, Small Group Church.

There were benefits and liabilities to each of these options. Attending a Chinese church would allow us more exposure to the language and local partners, yet the size of our family might also attract significant attention from the authorities – both to ourselves and to the church. Attending the legal International Fellowship would be stress-free and enable us to connect with other local expat families, but people we trusted had concerns about the teaching and worship. In the end, we joined our team leader and his family in attending the Small Group Church (SGC). Though this decision limited our contact with the Chinese church, it had the offsetting advantage of connecting us with a handful of other long-term, serious-minded missionary families – some of whom remain close friends to this day.

Sunday evenings were a bit more straightforward. With a team the size of ours – about a dozen adults and slightly more than a dozen children – getting everybody together for joint activities was a perpetual challenge. However, there was one event that was mandatory for every schedule: Sunday evening team worship. This arrangement guaranteed that every member of our team experienced solid teaching and worship at least once weekly. It also provided a consistent forum for fellowship and sharing information. There was only one challenge: two dozen people could not worship comfortably in even a spacious Chinese apartment. So where would we worship?

The answer proved to be one of the most amusing scenes of our early days in Chengdu. Not far from where most of us lived, there was a Western-themed restaurant whose owner was a Chinese believer. Her business was closed on Sundays, and so she was more than happy to rent her space to a group of Western Christians who wanted to meet for worship. Members of the mission would sit on chairs or even at the café tables. The pastor would lead worship and preach from behind the counter – standing between the cash register and the specialty coffee menu. More than once when I was officiating for our services, one of my sons would approach me and try to place an order.

Though a long way from being able to preach in Chinese, I had spent roughly six years preaching twice each Lord's Day during our ministry in Pennsylvania. This extensive experience, along with the accompanying deep archive of sermon notes, made me the obvious candidate to take over primary preaching responsibilities for our team. I was only too glad to accept this duty: in a context where I was a baby in everything else, it was encouraging to be able to find at least one sphere of reasonable competency.

Another task that fell to me during these early weeks between arrival and commencement of language school was the revision of our denomination's church-planting manual for translation and publication in Chinese. This was a somewhat complicated task. First, every reference to our home denomination's *Book of Church Order* – the operational manual for Presbyterian government, discipline, and worship – had to be replaced with references to the *Book of Church Order* used by the Chinese Presbyterian churches. Thankfully, the latter book had been translated into English for use by the associated missionaries. The second step in revising the church-planting manual was to identify and correct contextual discrepancies: things that made sense in a North American milieu but which would be meaningless in a Chinese context, or vice-versa. The third step was to augment the original text with new chapters and material specific to the Chinese context.

Given my previous experience as a church planter, Rob asked me to take the lead on this project. I redrafted each chapter, the English text was translated by a Chinese seminary student in America, and Rob served both as my advisor and the final editor of the translation. The final product was the firstfruit of what Rob and I both hoped would be a long collaboration – and a particular encouragement to me, especially after Rob reported that some of our national partners were enthusiastic about the new book's potential.

At the same time I was finding my niche in our team's ministry, my wife was likewise becoming increasingly comfortable amidst the Chengdu megalopolis. A day after I wrote the letter quoted above, she wrote the following in a letter of her own:

> Chengdu is a fun place to shop... For fresh fruits and vegetables, there are many store front shops and a larger "wet market" where they also sell fruits, vegetables, and

meat. Numerous convenience stores line every street... Wal-mart is where I have been shopping the most though. It is not like the Wal-marts we are used to at home in that the products they sell are, of course, geared more towards a Chinese market. But it is fun to see similar brands like "Great Value" and "Mainstays" and "Faded Glory"... If your load is too heavy to carry back, which mine often is, there are usually several motorized go-carts that can drive you and your bags back to your front gate – for less than a dollar. Or, you can simply leave everything in the cart and take the whole cart with you, wheel everything onto the elevator, drop everything off, and wheel the cart back to the front gate and leave it there. No need to take it the whole way back to the store. There is often a collection of carts by the gates (we have 2 gates) and someone must collect them at the end of the day... Sometimes people don't even bother returning carts at all. The kids thought it was hilarious one day when the elevator opened and an abandoned cart just sat there!

Though life was not without its challenges, by the end of our first full month in Chengdu we were moving beyond mere adjustment to our new city. Having finally found some time to exhale, we were now sensing – at a deeper level than we ever felt in Dongbei – the unique flavor of our context and mission. I wrote the following in a letter dated 24 February, 2018:

Next to a large pagoda, there were several women demonstrating their art of swirling long, dragon-headed ribbons in great spirals. One lady was even able to manage two ribbons simultaneously! If you look carefully, in the background you can see a high-rise apartment complex. In many ways, a picture like this epitomizes China – a society in which antiquity sits shoulder-to-shoulder with modernity.

Our work stands very much at this juxtaposition of old and new. On the one hand, news of Jesus first arrived in China in the early AD 600s – about 100 years before Saint Boniface began spreading the gospel and organizing the Church in Germany, and about 1000 years before any

Christians arrived in America. But on the other hand, it is only within the last 40 years or so that there has been a largescale movement of Church life in China from the countryside into the modern urban centers. The "old, old story" is permeating the gleaming metropolises of the East. Hundreds of millions of life stories are unfolding in these cities. Has there ever been such an opportunity for the Good Story to show so many a better Way?

A few weeks later, in mid-March, my wife's journal entry was a hymn of thanksgiving:

> Thankful that the Lord is our shield, our glory, and the lifter of our heads (Ps. 3). Thankful for the ladies on our team, their love for Christ, and their help and support for us. Thankful for the opportunity to serve Christ in this country. Thankful for a loving husband and children. Thankful for the opportunity to learn a new language. Thankful for even the small things: fresh fruit, tropical trees, singing birds, smiling faces, friendly dogs, new discoveries (kids able to "fish" and climb trees), good friends, time with those we love, good chocolate, ability to Skype and keep in touch regularly with those on the other side of the world. Thankful for my Lord and Savior, Jesus Christ, who guides and sustains me each and every day.

April 1, 2018 was a big day for our family: our first Easter in the eastern hemisphere! My wife's journal for the day captures our feelings vividly:

> Today is Easter Sunday! This is our first Easter in China. We worshipped this morning with our small group fellowship and afterwards enjoyed a meal together... It is an absolutely gorgeous spring day. The sun is out, the air is relatively clean. I am perched on a bench beneath a tree, remembering a bit those pleasant Sunday afternoons on our swing in Pennsylvania. I am sure it is much warmer here! I've spotted a few butterflies and am enjoying the sound of the birds, as well as the quiet chatter of Chinese folk as they pass by. Occasional car horns beep in the distance. Chengdu is a city full of life.

I like it here and am trying my best to call it home. I hope soon it will feel that way.

As I think of the life surrounding me, I am so thankful. Thankful for the lives of my family, dear friends, but most especially the new life I've received in Christ. Today we celebrate that He lives! As Mary's heart was full when she clung to her risen Lord, so my heart is full of joy. **He is Risen indeed!**

Chapter 17:
Plodding in Mandarin

A few weeks before beginning language classes at the Chinese university, I began reading an old biography of William Carey. In the course of my reading, I was bemused to read Carey's opinion regarding the ease of language acquisiton: "It is well known to require no very extraordinary talents to learn, in the space of a year, or two at most, the language of any people upon earth, so much of it at least as to be able to convey any sentiments we wish to their understandings."[1]

According to our team leader, who was a great admirer of Carey, something closer to five years was a more realistic timetable for acquiring proficiency in Chinese. Nevertheless, Carey's attitude was admirable – and his life story was a testimony to what is perhaps his most well-known saying: "Expect great things from God. Attempt great things for God." But my favorite quote from William Carey, which had hung near the door of my pastoral study in Pennsylvania, was more pragmatic: "I can plod. I can persevere in any definite pursuit. To this I owe everything."

---

1.   George Smith, *The Life of William Carey, Shoemaker and Missionary.* First published in 1885, this book is now in the public domain and available in numerous editions. I read a Kindle version.

I was excited to begin language classes – but also afraid. The week before my classes began, I wrote the following in a letter to my old friend and colleague, Paul:

> I am very much looking forward to taking up the task of learning the Chinese language. So much of our future usefulness depends on this; but even more (as you know), I've desired for twenty years to finally, really learn a second language.

> But I'm also somewhat afraid. As I've shared with you before, fear of failure is one of my most besetting sins. I don't think God sent me here to fail, of course – and I believe that it would be for my good if I did. Yet I will be happy once I begin to feel like I, my wife, and the kids are beginning to make real progress in the language.

The first day of formal classes was very short. The language program at my university had nine levels, and incoming students spent the first day taking a placement exam. Although the obsessive part of my personality simply wanted to begin at the first level so as to ensure that I missed nothing, Rob encouraged me to aim higher. Pointing out that both my wife and I had received quite a bit of informal Chinese study prior to enrollment, he suggested that I would do quite well in the placement test – and could probably begin at the second level.

The test results surprised both of us: I ended up qualifying for the fourth level. However, given the discrepancy between my ability in written Chinese (which was probably at the fourth level) and in spoken Chinese (closer to the second level), I ended up settling into the third-level classes. The spoken aspect of the classwork was challenging, and I always felt a bit behind some of my classmates. But the challenge was also a spur to keep plodding.

Re-entering university at mid-life would be interesting enough in any context. Imagine, then, how much more so it proved to be to enroll in language classes at a foreign university with classmates from all over the world.

At times, my language school seemed a collection of stereotypes. On one hand, there was a minority who were actually serious about learning Chinese. Though few would admit it, many of these were missionaries like myself (it is not difficult to recognize one's own kind). But the majority of our classmates seemed more interested in other things. Some were undergraduates on study abroad, focused primarily on finding the next party. Others were there for business: several of my classmates worked as fashion models, and another had an import/export business. A few others were at later stages of life: a piano player from New York, a photographer from Scandinavia, and an ex-soldier from Britain. But all of these had student visas – for the simple reason that our school paid little attention to either grades or extracurriculars, so long as students paid their tuition on time and fulfilled the minimal attendance requirements.

This mutually *suíbiàn* attitude between school and students proved to be both an advantage and a frustration. On the one hand, it allowed serious students like myself to shine. Simply by consistently attending class and doing the work, we acquired significant relational capital with the school's teachers and administrators. Although such capital is important in any culture, it is especially important in China – where such *guānxì* (lit. "relationship") can be the difference between an open or closed door. My family's long-term continuation in China depended not just on language acquisition, but also on the sustainability of our visa. If the teachers did not believe me to be a serious student, they would not feel respected. If the school did not see me making progress in Chinese, they might start wondering what I was actually doing with my time. Being a good student, therefore, had advantages quite apart from actually acquiring the language: it deflected suspicion and earned favor.

On the other hand, the lack of seriousness among many of my classmates fundamentally impeded the language learning process. Like all teachers, ours labored to instruct everybody in the classroom – even those who only attended half the time or paid only half-attention. I remember one incident, when our teacher called on a student who was sitting in the back of the classroom, ignoring the lesson and probably managing his business via his mobile phone. Her question was a sincere attempt to engage him in learning Chinese. He only laughed.

All of this meant that a significant number of my university hours were wasted, and by the end of the first semester I had come to a definite conclusion: though classes were useful for listening practice and asking questions, they could not drive my language progress. I could not leave the university without forfeiting my visa. But I would need to find other channels to really learn Chinese.

Thankfully, my wife and children had a better option for their language studies. Being covered by my visa as dependents, they did not have to attend any formal classes. Instead, we enrolled them at a private language school that employed the Growing Participator Approach – the very technique that we had learned in our cross-cultural training the previous year. Though they did not have as many hours per week to study as me, it was evident that they received superior instruction and made proportionally better progress. In fact, I was so impressed by the quality of my family's school that I eventually decided to enroll there – on top of my university classes – for extra tutoring.

My new one-on-one tutor, "Peter," turned out to be one of the most interesting men I met in China. Besides being a skilled teacher and translator, he was a dear Christian brother. When he learned that I was also a believer and a missionary, our relationship grew even closer – although it began with some awkward moments.

"I hate Calvinism," he said at the beginning of one of our earliest lessons. When I asked why, he told me about a young Chinese man with whom he had been speaking – a member of Early Rain, he told me – who had been coming on a little too strong in explaining his theological beliefs.

"Well, Peter," I said, taking a bit of a gamble, but wanting to be open with my friend, "you should probably know that I am a Calvinist."

"Yes, but that is your heritage," Peter said. "This guy didn't grow up in these beliefs. He only just learned these things. And now he is so "*jiāo'ào.*" The word *jiāo'ào* means "arrogant.""

"I see," I said. "Well, I believe you. This is sometimes a problem when people first begin to understand Calvinism. They get so excited about the teaching that they want to share it with everybody they know – and they are not too patient with people who do not agree."

Peter told me that was how the young man from Early Rain had been acting.

"When this happens," I continued, "in English we say that the person is in a 'cage stage.' They are too excited, and need to be put in a cage until they calm down."

Peter found this expression hilarious, and most of the tension dissipated...

"But the main idea of Calvinism," I pressed on, "is that God is really, really big, and that we are very, very small. When a person really comes to understand Calvinism, it should make them humble. Do you think I am *jiāo'ào*?"

"You are definitely not *jiāo'ào*!" he insisted.

Over the next year or so, Peter and I had many more interesting conversations. We discussed the relationship of human freedom to God's sovereignty, and at one point even began studying the biblical book of Romans together. In fact, we were so inclined to discuss theology that it was sometimes difficult to stay focused on Chinese lessons...

Peter remains a friend to this day, and we continue to help one another grow in both language and theology. Though now separated by half a world... still, together we can plod.

Chapter 18:
The Shadow of the Future

"The police were here this afternoon."

Thus my wife greeted me upon my arrival home, the Friday after my classes began...

Although there is probably no place in the world where an unexpected visit from the police would be welcome news, such tidings carried a particularly stressful tone in China. It's not because such visits are always negative. Sometimes they truly are just checking visa addresses for foreign residents, as required by Chinese law. Rather, the stress comes from the uncertainty: when the police are at the door, you always ask yourself, "Do they know?"

Uncertainty always creates stress, but not all uncertainty leads to deportation. In our case, the possibility was always there. We were missionaries living in a closed country. Legally, we were considered "religious spies." Although our American passports almost certainly could protect us from physical abuse or prolonged detention, they would not shield either ourselves or our children from intense interrogation followed by abrupt deportation. Try to imagine what it means to coach your children on what to say if they are ever questioned by the police about Daddy's activities...

Over time, we learned to live with the low-level stress associated with the ever-present possibility of being caught and deported. Just as missionaries in Africa have to accept a certain level of malaria parasites living in their bloodstream, so we came to accept a certain tenuousness and uncertainty over all of our days in China.

Nevertheless, it was still surprising that the police had visited us so soon in Chengdu. We had only just arrived, and I had yet to do anything that they might find even remotely "interesting." What then was the meaning of this visit? Had they somehow caught wind of my activities in Dongbei?

The whole affair turned out to be a case of mistaken identity. But this felt far less comforting than one might expect – for while the police were not looking for me, they were looking for our team leader, "Jack." My wife had misunderstood their inquiry at first because the Chinese name I was using at the time sounded almost identical to Jack's. Yet this fact did not explain why the police had come to our address – for tonal differences that confuse learners do not ruffle native speakers. Why then were they on our doorstep?

Here's what happened. Over the previous years, Jack and his family had lived in the same building into which we had just moved. In fact, their old apartment was in the same tower as ours – just a few floors higher. Then, sometime before our arrival, Jack's landlord abruptly cancelled his lease. Given the suddenness and lack of reasonable explanation, Jack suspected pressure from the authorities. This is standard operating procedure in China: whenever possible, Chinese authorities prefer indirect tactics to direct action. But Jack's landlord would admit nothing.

Although alarmed, my wife called Esther – who came over immediately to help translate. The police had heard that a foreign family had just moved into the building, and supposed that Jack's family had simply changed levels in the same towers. In the course of that conversation, Esther admitted to knowing Jack. Before realizing that she was an American citizen, one of the policemen scolded her for being associated with a "spy."

Wisely playing it cool, Esther offered to take the police to Jack's new apartment. It was less than a dozen blocks away, just across the line into the next city district. Though they had called him a spy, the officers did not seem interested in actually confronting Jack – for they declined Esther's offer, took a photo with my wife to prove they had made the visit, and departed without further questions. After that, we all hoped that Jack and his family would receive no further molestation.

It was not to be. But before explaining what happened to Jack, it will help to have a bit more information on the nature and work of our team...

We moved to Chengdu in order to join a team dedicated to mentoring and training an emerging, organizing, confessional Presbyterian denomination in China. Although the urbanization of the house church movement in China had been underway for many years,[1] the Reformed branch of that movement was still relatively young.[2] One of the flagship churches in this fledgling Reformation movement – indeed, one of the most famous house churches in China – was Early Rain Covenant Church in Chengdu, led by Pastor Wang Yi.[3]

Though Early Rain was the most famous church in Chengdu, it was by no means the only congregation with Reformation-minded commitments. Indeed, an entire network of Reformed congregations had formed in the city and its surrounding region – "Huaxi Presbytery." Together, the churches of the presbytery had formed a seminary – Western China Covenant Theological Seminary (WCCTS). In addition to the seminary, there were other encouraging facets of the Reformed movement in southwest China. These included Christian publishing as well as Christian primary and secondary education initiatives.

Perhaps most striking of all was Huaxi Presbytery's decision to operate aboveground. This was a significant departure from the *modus operandi* of traditional unregistered churches. Ever since the days of Deng Xiaoping, house churches in China had been permitted a modest, but slowly increasing level of unofficial

---

1. For more information on the urbanization of Chinese Christianity, see Brent Fulton, *China's Urban Christians: A Light That Cannot Be Hidden* (Eugene, OR: Pickwick, 2015).

2. See Bruce P. Baugus, ed., *China's Reforming Churches* (Grand Rapids: Reformation Heritage, 2014).

3. One of the best available profiles of Early Rain and Wang Yi is contained in Ian Johnson, *Souls of China: the Return of Religion after Mao* (New York: Pantheon, 2017).

toleration – a sort of "don't ask, don't tell" policy. But there were certain firm parameters within which all unregistered churches were expected to operate – four basic rules. These were: 1) don't draw too much attention or get too big, 2) don't criticize the government, 3) don't associate with foreigners, and 4) don't try to form large-scale networks. Violating any of these rules could bring trouble.

But the Huaxi churches were not just breaking one of the rules. They were breaking all of them. They actively promoted their ministries through social media, and Pastor Wang Yi was a vocal critic of Xi Jinping. They welcomed foreigners to teach at their schools and seminary, and they were assisting other forming presbyteries across the country.

How had the Huaxi churches gotten away with such defiance for so long? They had taken an active role in bringing disaster relief in the wake of the horrifying Sichuan earthquake in May 2008, a 7.9 magnitude earthquake in which almost 90,000 people were listed as dead or missing. Such service had won them a significant amount of public goodwill. This goodwill, combined with the more relaxed Sichuan culture generally and the distance from Beijing, created a remarkable opportunity for large-scale, surprisingly public ministry.

Though we did not know it before coming to Chengdu, this period of unprecedented Christian liberty in southwest China was swiftly drawing to a close. The revised "Regulations on Religious Affairs" issued by Xi's government in September 2017 possessed real teeth, and Pastor Wang's willingness to criticize the "core leader" made him an obvious target. On 11 March, 2018, Pastor Wang was quoted by name in a *New York Times* article criticizing Xi's abolition of presidential term limits and self-aggrandizing constitutional revision: "Abolishing the term limit on the leader of state does not make a leader but a usurper. Writing a living person's name into the Constitution is not amending the Constitution but destroying it."[4]

Such rhetoric made confrontation almost inevitable, and this seemed to be Pastor Wang's intent. A friend who worked closely

---

4.   Chris Buckley and Steven Lee Myers, "China's Legislature Blesses Xi's Indefinite Rule," *New York Times*, 11 March, 2018. https://www.nytimes.com/2018/03/11/world/asia/china-xi-constitution-term-limits.html (accessed 20 October, 2020).

with one of Early Rain's ministries confirmed this to me around the time of the *Times* article. Pastor Wang Yi aimed to provoke the government to act decisively: either to back down decisively from any restriction of the Chinese Church, or to crack down in such a way that would show the world its true colors.

Though the decisive response would not come until 9 December, on 1 February – the very day on which the new religious regulations officially went into effect – the school where Jack taught English informed him that he was going to be laid off. A week later, Jack and I were together in a coffee shop when the school called again. They informed him that they were cancelling his visa with immediate effect. To save face for both parties, he was being asked to resign the next day. Again, it was an indirect assault – but the real culprit was clear. By the end of the week, Jack and his family were on a plane...

What had Jack done to attract such attention? He was closely connected to Pastor Wang Yi.

Jack's visa troubles began almost the day our family arrived in Chengdu. Eventually, through maneuvers that were as clever as they are complicated, Jack's family was able to return to our city for a short time. Nevertheless, a shadow was spreading over our mission – a shadow far darker than Chengdu's usual unicloud.

Chapter 19:
Journey to the West

In late March, Jack invited me to accompany him and Rob to the graduation ceremony for Western China Covenant Theological Seminary. Though I could only catch words and a few phrases of what was said, the event affected me tremendously. Reflecting on it, I wrote the following in our next letter to friends and family:

> I never expected to be living the life we now live... Consequently, times like these frequently feel a bit surreal. Yet I went away with a greater experiential sense of the importance, the joy, and the reality of the global church and our service to them. Presence communicates more than words or even photographs can express.

In early April, we celebrated our first Easter in China – our first Easter in the eastern hemisphere. The joy of this occasion was magnified by its sharp contrast with a traditional Chinese festival that occurred just five days later – *Qīngmíngjié* ("Tomb-Sweeping Day"). On Tomb-Sweeping Day, Chinese people gather at the tombs of their ancestors to clean the grave markers, present offerings of food and drink, and burn paper money.

On the day before the festival, I committed a significant personal gaffe. As I left class that day, I wished my teacher

"Qīngmíngjié Kuàilè!" ("Happy Tomb-Sweeping Day!"). Though not offended, my teacher kindly yet quickly informed me that Tomb-Sweeping Day is not a holiday regarding which you can use the well-wishing phrase *kuàilè* ("happy") – because on this day, people are very sad. The incident was a reminder to me that, though technically a holiday, there is a cold, hopeless undercurrent to the tradition.

With Tomb-Sweeping Day creating a long weekend for our city and our labors, a number of our teammates decided to leave Chengdu and visit the mountains in the northwest part of Sichuan province. This part of our province was particularly interesting: though it technically remains in Sichuan, it is culturally and ethnically a Tibetan region. We stayed in a tiny city nestled amidst the Minshan Mountains. According to our guides, the Minshan Mountains could be regarded as part of the eastern edge of the Himalayas, broadly defined.

Beyond the cultural interest, the opportunity to breathe fresh air and hike to nearly 10,000 feet – in the eastern foothills of the Himalayas, no less – proved a bracing balm to our team. It was a good reminder to us that there is far more to China than its megacities and its dominant Han culture. To this day, one of my favorite photos from China is a picture of our sons standing on a mountaintop watchtower; it looks like a scene lifted from Tolkien.

Balancing the sweetness of our mountain ascent, however, was the darkness into which we descended while visiting a Tibetan Buddhist monastery. I wrote the following account:

> We saw the hermitages for the regular monks, the yellow-walled homes for the lamas (who are believed to be living incarnations of gods), and some of us were even permitted to walk through the temple during one of its services. We saw rows of prayer wheels, including a massive one hanging in its own special structure.
>
> Although there is a somewhat fashionable mystique surrounding this belief system in the West, I came away from the monastery with a sense of profound sadness. The inside of the temple was very dark, and the doors of the shrines are covered in skulls. Our guide even took us for a walk around the perimeter of one building –

JOURNEY TO THE WEST

which appears to be covered in graffiti. But when you look closely, you see that it is not graffiti, but hash marks people are making as they circled the building for the thousandth, or ten thousandth, time.

Why were they making so many trips around the shrine, and why did they have to keep such careful count? Because after paying a hefty fee to consult the lama, they were told that they could earn good karma by walking 1,000, 2,000, or even 10,000 times around the shrine. This is also why people count prayer beads and come to turn the prayer wheels – because they believe that by turning the wheels they can earn the same amount of spiritual points that they would have earned by repeating a special mantra several thousand times.

...I would encourage you to weep rather than to scorn. Do you realize that for millions of people, this is the only "hope" to which they have ever been exposed? It is a system of fear – and there is never certainty that one has ever done enough to earn a better rebirth.

I share this story of the monastery with all of you not to make any of us proud, but rather to make all of us humble. If you happen to have been born in a family or society that knows the gospel, you should thank God right now – because if we had been born there, it is possible that every one of us would be making those hopeless treks to pay the lama and circle the shrine. In fact, many of us still cling to a Westernized form of karma, where we think we can earn God's blessing or make up for our sins by being a good person, doing good deeds, or giving money to charity.

Even those who know Christ often fall into this trap. I have known more than one Christian who acted as though their relationship to God depended on their intellectual knowledge of doctrine (and their ability to criticize others). I have known others who acted as though their relationship with God depended on the purity of their faith or their prayers... all of it is self-salvation. All of it is from the Enemy. It is not the solution; it is the problem. God didn't send His Son to earth to give us a prayer wheel or a scorecard. He sent Him to be our Door. That is why the gospel is good news, not good advice.

My wife had a similar reaction to the monastery. In her journal, she recorded the following:

> Our tour guide took us to a Tibetan Buddhist monastery. This was a sad place. As we walked through the temple, the robed monks and young boys said their chants, their "prayers" for atonement... One could feel the oppression and evil inside here: I prayed for these men and young boys – that they would one day know and understand that they cannot save themselves – it is only by grace through faith in Christ. May that one day be revealed to them and may they embrace the One who truly saves...

> Upon further reflection, these people (as the Israelites) "pursue a law that would lead to righteousness" and "did not succeed in reaching that law. Why? Because they did not pursue it by faith, but as if it were based on works," (Rom. 9:31-32).

> "My heart's desire and prayer to God for them is that they may be saved," (Rom. 10:1). May they "confess with their mouths that Jesus is Lord and believe in their hearts that God raised Him from the dead – they will be saved," (Rom. 10:9). May they "call on the name of the Lord," (Rom. 10:13).

> Lord, may you send preachers to these people! For "How then will they call on him in whom they have not believed? And how are they to believe in him of whom they have never heard? And how are they to hear without someone preaching? And how are they to preach unless they are sent?" (Rom. 10:14-15) "So faith comes from hearing, and hearing through the word of Christ," (Rom. 10:17).

Like the seminary graduation, our journey to the west deepened our sense of China's need. "Presence communicates more than words or even photographs can express."

Chapter 20:
The World Cup and the Terracotta Army

Spring and summer of 2018 blossomed with encouragements for our family and for our work. We were learning the language bit by bit, the weather was warming after the chill damp of winter, and even life in a small apartment amidst a big city seemed increasingly comfortable. In mid-April, my wife wrote the following to a friend in Pennsylvania:

> It is nice having a smaller place to take care of. We have a vacuum cleaner that doesn't work well, so I use the broom mostly. The boys help out with dishes everyday, so that has been a blessing. I thought I would really miss my dishwasher, but I find handwashing dishes to be relaxing. We have a very small clothes dryer that will only dry, of course, very small loads. So most of the time I hang clothes out to dry on our balcony. Again, something I thought would be hard and take a lot of extra time, but it doesn't really, and I enjoy hanging clothes...
>
> I think city life is growing on me. Our city does have a lot of trees and greenery, which is nice. No dandelions though, so feel free to pick one for me! I love how conviently close everything is (fresh produce stands, bakeries, convenience stores, restaurants) and how easy it is to travel, once you can figure out where you

are going and how to get there. I enjoy taking the metro and bus – probably the best for longer distance trips – but most of the time, I just walk to stores around our neighborhood.

My wife was not the only one finding more and more to enjoy about life in Chengdu. Our daughter rejoiced when we agreed to "babysit" a cat for another missionary family returning to Great Britain on furlough. Though neither family realized it at the time, "babysit" in this case turned out to mean "adopt indefinitely" – for the family was never able to return, and we ended up keeping the cat until we departed from China. In addition to this feline advent, our daughter was again delighted when she and I were invited to attend a "Daddy-Daughter Dance" organized by the local expat community. This proved to be a party of special magnificence for her – a social debutant for our little girl.

Shortly thereafter, our second son purchased a bicycle from one of our friends in the city. When he and I walked it to a local shop to have the tires inflated, we expected a bit of an adventure. Would we be able to find the shop, based on our friend's directions? Would I be able to communicate adequately with the *lǎobǎn* (shopkeeper)? What we did not expect was for one of the tires to explode as it was being inflated – with a bang that grabbed the attention of the entire busy street! Thankfully, the shop carried extra tubes and everything was replaced and inflated in under ten minutes – and for less than four dollars. My son rode his bicycle around our complex for the remainder of the afternoon. He was, that day, almost certainly the happiest boy in Chengdu. Thinking of him a week or so later, I wrote in my prayer journal: "Grant that he would think of You today as the 'God of bicycles' – the Creator of something he enjoys so much."

As our comfort in navigating our next context grew, our functional map of our city expanded. A highlight of this expansion for my eldest son was our discovery of, and subsequent return visits to, the "Digital City" – a multi-level electronics shop that we could get to by the metro subway or by bus. The lowest level of this shop was a slick retail center full of polished displays and aggressive salespeople. From here, one could ascend via escalator or elevator to upper levels containing less shine in the displays and more apathy from the clerks. Our favorite floors were the middle ones – a giant electronics flea market in which one could find everything from the latest solid state hard drives to the most primitive adapters. For the geekishly inclined, it was a little slice of heaven.

Another regular encouragement upon our settlement in Chengdu were the monthly packages sent by my parents. Sometimes these included books that we could not obtain in China: theological books for my work, and eventually an entire set of hymnals for our family. Almost always they also contained either coffee roasted by my father, or candy purchased by my mother. On occasion, however, the packages would bring us something a little more exotic. For example, my parents once sent our daughter a big plastic car for her toy cat. This particular package took a long time to arrive – not because of its contents, but because the US Postal Service had mistakenly first shipped it to Iceland!

A big step in cross-cultural courage came in early May, when my eldest son and I went together for the first time to a Chinese barbershop. When we lived in Pennsylvania, I had handled all the haircuts for myself and my sons at home: it saved money, and it wasn't difficult. But after relocating to Chengdu, I had begun going to Jack's barber: the cost was inexpensive, and the opportunity to connect with local people was invaluable. The first time I went, Jack had accompanied me and told me exactly what to say. This time, however, my son and I went without a translator. Thankfully, we managed to communicate clearly enough... and came away looking pretty sharp. For the remainder of our time in Chengdu, my two oldest boys and I would regularly return to this shop – and I would try my best to use the opportunity to practice my Chinese with the husband and wife who worked there.

Two more events from this period deserve particular notice as encouraging milestones. The first of these came in June, when I was asked to speak at a married couples' retreat being facilitated by one of the Huaxi churches. The teammate who arranged the invitation assured me that I would have a translator for the primary portion of my talk. However, he and his wife both suggested that I should try to give a self-introduction in Mandarin – and without any assistance.

The prospect of addressing the subject of marriage was not itself overly daunting. I had gathered a baseline of marriage-related material in the course of pre-marital counseling during my previous ministry. Additional resources had recently come to my attention that could be obtained digitally. With my wife's assistance, I developed a keynote talk entitled, "Lessons Learned after Sixteen Years of Marriage." This all came together smoothly.

The self-introduction in Mandarin was more intimidating. However, I knew that my teammate and his wife were correct to suggest it. Years prior, when I was preparing to conduct open-air evangelism on the university campus in Pennsylvania, an older evangelist had told me: at some point, you just have to make a first go. The same was true now. When it came to using Mandarin in public, the first time would have to come sometime. A self-introduction at the married couples' retreat seemed as good an opportunity as any: the crowd would be modest in size and gracious in spirit. I agreed to try.

The event itself went well. Though I was nervous to make the attempt, the self-introduction in Chinese went reasonably well; my translator told me she was positively impressed by my level in the language. The subsequent, translated address went even better. Seminar participants expressed appreciation, and the beginnings of personal relationships with several members of the local church were established. Overall, it was highly encouraging.

In addition to providing my first experience using Mandarin in public, the married couples' retreat also introduced me to something that became very important to my family that summer: the 2018 World Cup. The night I arrived at the retreat, I was invited to watch one of the opening matches with the conference participants. Not wanting to be anti-social, I agreed – but without any particular interest. The event turned out to be another semi-surreal experience: was I really here, on the far side of the world, surrounded by Chinese brothers and sisters, watching Mexico upset Germany? It was the first time I had ever watched a soccer match on television, yet in that moment I came to understand why the sport has such global appeal. Returning to Chengdu the next day, I shared my experience with my wife and kids. We tried watching a match together as a family – and were hooked.

The other encouraging waypoint from this period came in July, when my second son celebrated his birthday. We have a tradition in our family that when our children reach the age of twelve, I take them on a special trip in order to have some important conversations about growing up. Neither my son nor I had forgotten about this tradition, and despite the fact that we were now living in a foreign country where travel was less simple, we were determined that his trip should move forward. The question was: where, and how, to go?

We decided to travel to Xi'an via high-speed rail. Though we received assistance in purchasing tickets and arranging a guide to take us to the Terracotta Army, we traveled unaccompanied. It was in this regard that the trip to Xi'an was a milestone in our life and ministry in China: the first time we had traveled in-country without more experienced assistance. Could we manage?

By God's grace, we not only managed – the trip was marvelous in the full sense of the word. As my wife and I had done two years earlier, so now my second son and I saw the Nestorian Stone and the Terracotta Army – two of ancient China's greatest wonders. We explored the Muslim Quarter and ate delicious foods: fresh shish kabobs, watermelon juice, and fried bananas. But the highlight for us both was to ride bicycles around the top of the ancient city wall. It was the most joy either he or I had felt since our family moved to China – one of those formative experiences that shapes both young and old alike. How many kids from Pennsylvania could say they've biked atop a city wall that is older than the United States?

Little by little – *mànman lái*, as the Chinese would say – our family was gaining its feet.

Chapter 21:
The Giant Family Enclosure

No matter how acclimated to China we became, our family never ceased to attract attention when we went out together. This had been true from our earliest days in Dongbei, and it continued throughout our time in Chengdu. We were frequently photographed or videoed. Elderly women liked to pat our children on the head. Wherever we went as a family, we could never simply blend in.

One word we heard frequently was, *"Wàiguórén!"* ("Foreigner!") Most of the time it came from the lips of small Chinese children, who – like children in any culture – naturally pointed out to their parents those who looked different from themselves. It never felt malicious. Yet it could be wearying, especially for our children. Who really wants to be noticed all the time, everywhere they go?

Eventually, our kids learned to bear their new celebrity with relatively good grace – if perhaps with an occasional touch of mischievousness. For example, one day while we were at a shopping mall, a child pointed to our second son.

"Wàiguórén!" he cried.

Without missing a beat, our son pointed back.

"Zhōngguórén!" he replied in Chinese ("Chinese person!").

The boy seemed surprised. His mother laughed.

Our ultimate celebrity experience came on 1 June 2018, when our entire family was invited to attend an "International Children's Day" celebration at one of the city's elite middle schools. Our invitation came from the two local boys we had hosted in our Pennsylvania home several years prior to coming to China. Both of them attended this school, and one in particular was very excited to bring his American "Dad" and "Mom," along with all of their children, to his school festivities. Not knowing what to expect, we accepted.

As it turned out, Children's Day is rather a big deal in China. To mark the occasion, the middle school where our Chinese "sons" attended held a giant outdoor festival. They converted the sports field into a festival park, and each of the school's clubs manned a booth displaying their interests. There were dancing robots, ping pong competitions, traditional calligraphy tables, and even a club for "sport stacking" – a game in which cups are stacked into pyramids and then unstacked as quickly as possible.

As the only *wàiguórén* on campus, our arrival at the middle school caused more than a little stir. Students thronged around our family, and we were led in procession around the field to visit each booth. Our eldest son served as judge in an English spelling competition, our second son won a set of ping pong paddles, and I tried my hand at calligraphy. Students, parents, and teachers were so kind to us; nevertheless, it was a little overwhelming for our clan. Later that night, as we enjoyed supper with our Chinese boys and their friends, one of the moms was incredulous when I told her Americans did not celebrate Children's Day.

"Búhuìba!" she exclaimed – which translates to something like, "Inconceivable!"

As amazing as American "neglect" of Children's Day might be to the Chinese, more amazing by far to us was how the Lord had created this connection between our family and these two Chinese students. Long before we had ever imagined living in China, let alone Chengdu, God had sent two boys from our future city to our home in Pennsylvania. Even now, years later, it remains one of the most extraordinary providences of our connection to China.

Apart from our visit to the middle school, our big family had an even greater impact on our children's Chinese tutor, "Lucy." One day, when I arrived at the language school for my own supplemental tutoring with Peter, Lucy told me just how much the Lord had used my wife and children to work in her own heart.

"When I first met your family, I did not like children," she said. "I did not want children."

I nodded. "Really?"

"Yes, but your family changed me," she continued. "Now, when I am married, I want to have many children!"

In addition to working as a Chinese tutor, Lucy was also a student at the college associated with Early Rain Covenant Church. She was studying education, and was interested to know more about how my wife homeschooled our children. So she came to our house one day and observed my wife teaching the kids – a sort of homeschooling "open house."

Lucy was not the only local Christian interested in homeschooling. As China's new religious regulations increased pressure on unregistered Christian schools, an increasing number of Chinese Christian families began exploring the possibility of homeschooling. But even among serious Christians, homeschooling was relatively uncharted territory in China. Printed curriculum was not easy to come by, and experienced voices were even more rare. Here was an area where the Lord had clearly opened a door of ministry for my wife.

Later that year, about two weeks before Thanksgiving, my wife and one of the single ladies on our team (herself an experienced homeschooling educator) hosted a meeting for local Chinese parents interested in homeschooling. They answered questions, offered encouragement, and brainstormed on the best ways to further equip Chinese Christians in this new and important endeavor.

Experiences like these are a strong reminder to us just how often God works in directions orthogonal to those we expect. In coming to China, my wife and I had expected the size of our family to present us with challenges. We had not expected it to change the life of a Chinese sister. Likewise, our decision to continue homeschooling had arisen more out of necessity than anything else, since neither we nor our missions organization could afford to send five children to Chengdu's international school. We had not expected our educational necessity to become a ministry opportunity. The Lord, however, had planned it all along.

But the Lord didn't just use our large family experience to serve others. He also used it to shape us. In our American culture of origin, we had always been part of the ethnic majority. As such, there was no way we could ever know what it was like for foreigners or minorities living in our society. Our sojourn in China changed all this. Though our experience as *wàiguórén* in China was considerably more privileged than that of immigrants and minorities in America, nevertheless it gave our family a real and enduring taste of what it means to live your whole life in the constant awareness of being different – an outsider.

As important as this lesson was and remains, our status as *wàiguórén* could also create moments of memorable humor. One such instance came during our very last weeks in China in August 2019, when my son and I went to register our passports and addresses at the local police station. This was something that has to be done every time a foreigner returns from outside the country, and it is a relatively routine process. What wasn't routine, however, was the scene that unfolded...

"Is that boy French?" I heard one of the policewomen ask her colleague, pointing to my teenage son who had accompanied me to the *pàichūsuǒ* ("local police station").

"No, his Dad is an American," came the gruff reply from another policewoman. All the officers on duty that day in the registration office were ladies.

Disbelieving, the officer came around the desk and walked up to my son. "Are you French?" she asked him in Chinese.

"We're Americans," I answered in Chinese.

"Can I touch your hair?" she next asked my son, who quickly shook his head negatively.

"He's a bit shy," I told her. It was easier than trying to explain that Americans generally don't allow strangers to pet their hair...

"Is his mother French?" she asked me.

At this point, I decided to have some fun. My wife had studied French at university, so I said quite honestly, "His mother can speak French."

"Ah!" said several officers at once, clearly now feeling validated in their suspicions. When I showed them a picture of my whole family a minute later, they pointed to my wife.

"She looks French."

As we left the *pàichūsuǒ* that day, I struggled to contain my laughter until we passed through the gate. My son was far less amused...

"I'm never going to hear the end of this, am I?"

I flashed him a mischievous grin. "My little French boy..."

Writing to the Corinthians more than two thousand years ago, the apostle Paul spoke of himself and his fellow apostles as "a spectacle to the world, to angels, and to men. We are fools for Christ's sake," (1 Cor. 4:9-10). When he wrote these words, Paul was almost certainly brooding on images far more serious than our incident at the *pàichūsuǒ*. Yet in a small way, our experience resonated: to live for Jesus as *wàiguórén* in China was to be a "spectacle" and to sometimes look and feel like "fools for Christ's sake."

The Bible says that all believers are "sojourners and exiles" (1 Pet. 2:11), "strangers and exiles on the earth... seeking a homeland," (Heb. 11:13-14). Believers who never have the blessing of living for an extended period in a foreign culture may struggle to keep this in perspective. But for those of us to whom the Lord has given such a privilege, experiences such as our interaction with the policewomen that day – and the less amusing reminders we faced everyday in China – underlined this important spiritual reality:

We are strangers and foreigners in this life, no matter where we live. Home is neither where we are from, nor where we live. Home is simply where God calls us to be. Until we enter the new creation, we will always be *wàiguórén* – not just in China, but even in America.

As amusing as was the incident from the end of our time in China, the most defining *wàiguórén* moment for us as a family came a few weeks before Thanksgiving in 2018. My in-laws had come to visit us, and as part of showing them our city we took them to the Giant Panda Base. Toward the end of our time in the massive park, having walked great distances and braved dense crowds of spectators surrounding the "giant panda enclosure," our family was taking a snack break near some benches.

While we ate our snack and drank our water, my wife and I began noticing that Chinese visitors to the park were slowing down as they approached us. Smartphones were coming out, pointed in our direction. My stepfather-in-law is a tall man, and my mother-in-law had lighter hair. Adding the two of them to our crew further increased our visibility. Once again we were being recorded, our pictures beaming out over Chinese social media to the fascination of thousands…

But we didn't get frustrated. I turned to my wife and chuckled. "We are the 'Giant Family Enclosure.'"

Chapter 22:
Lots of Tomorrows

Though we did not realize it at the time, late summer 2018 retrospectively appears to have been the apogee of our ministry in China – not only for my family, but also for our mission. For years, the denomination through which we served had only two ordained ministers in China: Bruce and Rob. But with the coming of our family in 2017 to serve with Rob, and with the arrival of "Chip" and his family in spring 2018 to serve with Bruce, the mission in China had reached a long-desired goal of having two ordained men in each station. This wasn't a mere numerical aspiration. Rather, as Presbyterians, we believed that ministers should operate as a plurality (more than one) rather than in isolation. After all, both our Lord and the early church had sent men out in pairs (Mark 6:7, Luke 10:1, Acts 13:2-3).

As our mission expanded, we also needed to make certain adjustments. Our two stations labored in two significantly different contexts. Our work in Dongbei focused on more frontline labors: evangelism and church-planting. Our work in Chengdu focused its activities more behind-the-scenes: mentoring, publishing, and training. Moreover, whereas the churches we served in Dongbei remained underground, the Huaxi churches in Chengdu conducted their ministry more openly. With this difference in both context and focus, and with the new blessing of a plurality of leaders in each station, it made sense to rewrite our bylaws to provide each station with a prudent degree of operational autonomy. This task fell to me.

Another task which our mission assigned to me was the drafting of our five-year plan for 2019–2023. Although such plans always need to be taken with a grain of salt – particularly in China, where things can change so rapidly and unpredictably, as we would all soon so grievously learn – they nonetheless aid a mission in focusing both its overall strategy and its day-to-day activity. In addition, they provide a tangible basis for periodic assessment and accountability.

With our two stations operating with new strength under new bylaws, and with a new five-year plan ready for review, the leaders of our denomination's foreign missions committee – Barnabas and James – made a plan to come to China in person to meet with all of us together. They would travel first to Dongbei, to meet with and encourage the station members there. After a few days, Rob and I would fly up so that the full mission leadership could meet together. After this, Barnabas and James would return with us to Chengdu to meet with and encourage our families.

The visit was not without its moments: Dongbei had experienced some flooding and extreme summer heat, and there was a day without electricity in Chengdu. Nevertheless, our meetings went relatively well. While in Dongbei, I was able to have coffee with the former student whom I had baptized the previous winter. That trip was also my first opportunity to meet Chip and his family face-to-face. When Barnabas and James reached Chengdu, they brought counsel for me, gifts for our children, and a new shipment of medicine for my wife – whose chronic illness had resurfaced since our move to Chengdu.

Before returning to the United States, Barnabas and James presented our mission with a parting gift: knowing the importance of strong relationships even across far-flung stations, the foreign missions committee would pay for a whole-mission retreat in February 2019. Bruce and Chip, along with their families, would fly to Chengdu. There was to be no special ministry activities; the goal was simply for our families to enjoy time together. For my wife, who had not yet met Chip or his family, this was an encouraging prospect.

Another encouragement for our family followed fast on the heels of this visit. The day after Barnabas and James departed, our entire family boarded the high-speed rail for a week's vacation in Yunnan province. Though we always enjoy seeing new places, our family was just as excited to visit Yunnan because it meant we would meet some new friends.

The story of how we came to meet "Nathaniel" and "Verity" is a fine example of just how small the world can be. Just prior to our departure for China in August 2017, I had completed a short monograph and submitted it to a friend of mine who works in Christian publishing. He could make no promises, but agreed to pass it on for review. I thanked him for the consideration, we moved to China, and the matter was more or less forgotten.

Then in April 2018, I received an email communication from a pastor connected with the publisher for whom my friend works. Not only was the pastor pleased to recommend my little booklet for publication, he also shared with me that he had some dear friends in China – a family close to us not just in terms of geography, but also in terms of age and theology. Would it be okay to put us in contact? We agreed eagerly, and the subsequent introduction led to a correspondence which in turn led to an invitation – and ultimately to our first family vacation in China.

The name "Yunnan" means "Southern Clouds" – a name that proved accurate to our impressions of the province. Although it is further south than Sichuan province, the climate in Yunnan was cooler during our visit due to the fact that the city where we stayed sat at a higher elevation than Chengdu. There was much culture and history to explore in Yunnan: 26 of China's 56 ethnic groups can be found in the province, and in the provincial capital there is a museum exhibition celebrating the "Flying Tigers" – a volunteer group of American pilots who served with the Chinese Air Force in World War II.

But more delightful than all of this was the opportunity to meet Nathaniel, Verity, and their family. Their two daughters shared some common interests with our children and played well together. Verity shared a love of coffee with my wife and me, and did an excellent job throughout our time together of making sure that we never went too long without a well-brewed cup. Nathaniel and I had much to discuss, of course, and in the course of our visit he introduced me to the use of "Mobike" – an incredibly affordable and convenient system for bicycle ride-sharing available in almost every major Chinese city.

All in all, we could not have asked for a more refreshing trip – or more encouraging new friends. Like us, but unlike most of our closest colleagues back in Chengdu, Nathaniel and Verity were both Westerners – and like us they had brought their family to China in mid-life. For the first time, we felt like we had found people who could fully relate to our situation and experience. As we returned to Chengdu in mid-August, therefore, both my wife and I felt a great hope for the future of this relationship.

Yet it was not just for our immediate family, nor even for our denominational family, that we had high hopes in late summer. Our local, inter-denominational team in Chengdu also seemed to be gaining momentum. Jack and his family were back in the States for six months on furlough, but in late August Jack invited both Rob and I to join him in Taipei, Taiwan, for a meeting of representatives from seminaries across China. While there, one of our keynote speakers said something that I have carried with me ever since.

In discussing the nature of theological training, the speaker said that churches in the Reformed and Presbyterian tradition are pretty good about training future church leaders in correct doctrine ("orthodoxy"): we have our systematic theology, and we teach it systematically. He went on to suggest that we are also reasonably successful in training future church leaders in correct practice ("orthopraxy"): we know that ideas have consequences, and we train our pastors to live and teach the same. So far, so good.

However, our teacher that day in Taipei also drew a bead on a significant failure in many Reformed and Presbyterian churches: we are not good at either modeling or training men in living and serving with the right attitude or right spirit ("orthopathos"). Why do too many of our ministers seem out of touch with the realities of regular life for ordinary people? Why do we so often fall for the temptation to chase hobby horses rather than minister grace to the lost and broken? To reinforce his point, the speaker suggested that the first question for any man coming for ordination should be this: when is the last time you shared the gospel with an addict – a person deeply broken and enslaved by sin?

This was an edgy suggestion for a room full of academics, but it hit its mark. Our speaker was not fixating on one particular category of sin. Rather, he was honing in on a common gap in our ministerial training. What does it profit a church if it should gain the whole world of doctrinal knowledge, but forfeit its soul? Although our speaker's words were convicting, the shift in paradigm he presented was both positive and encouraging.

Perhaps the whole of this period can be summarized in words my wife and I received from a surprise visitor in mid-August. We had first met "Don" years earlier, while we were still serving the church back in the Pennsylvania university city – and when he visited our church with his brother's family during furlough. At that time, Don had been a China missionary for decades. Neither he nor we could have ever expected that we would someday share a meal in Chengdu. Yet that is exactly what happened one evening: Don and his family were passing through Chengdu, and we got together for dinner.

While we were together, I asked Don to tell us anything he had learned that he wished he had known when he was beginning his life abroad. The first thing he said was, "There are lots of tomorrows." When we said goodnight after dinner that warm summer night, it seemed hard to disagree. The future of our life and ministry in China seemed bright. We had great expectations – and there seemed to be lots of tomorrows.

Chapter 23:
Falling Leaves

Despite the fact that falling leaves presage barren limbs, autumn has ever been my favorite season. In late August, I wrote the following to a friend in the States:

> Your hopes for a "good crisp fall" make me think of cool air, colored leaves, starry nights, and the smell of woodsmoke... no matter how far we travel, the image of a leaf-strewn path through the woods during a Pennsylvania autumn will ever be one of the enduring images in my heart's gallery.

As our one and only autumn season in southwest China drew near, our expectations were not substantially unlike those of our friends in the West. School would begin, the weather would cool, and soon we would all fall into our customary fall routine. Regarding the kids' schooling, we were pretty optimistic about some adjustments we were making: our eldest son was beginning a highly recommended online high school, and our second son was joining a math and science co-op being taught by one of our teammates.

Outside of school, our family spirits were also generally high. Our third son had developed a taste for *jiǎozi* (Chinese dumplings) – an affordable food for which he and I would regularly go questing during our weekly "special time." Meanwhile, our extroverted youngest son had made a number of expat friends – many of whom lived in our own or the neighboring *xiǎoqū* ("gated apartment complex"). Though not quite as adventurous as her older brothers, our daughter also enjoyed playing outdoors – or going on "Daddy dates" to a local cat café. Rob and I had even worked out a scheme whereby we could stream college football games from the States...

However, as the leaves began to fall, it was also increasingly clear that not all was well with my wife's health. For more than ten years, she had suffered from a chronic medical condition. Properly medicated, this condition did not affect her ability to function or her quality of life. In her case, however, there was a particular challenge: most medicines had failed, leaving us with only two known options. She had begun the first of these in 2016, with remarkable success. Prior to agreeing to come to China, therefore, we had investigated whether we would be able to continue this prescription while living abroad. Every indicator was positive, and so we made what arrangements we could: we carried medicine with us when we moved, we had a six-month supply brought to us in Dongbei, and we made plans to seek out and establish care with a new specialist as soon as we settled in Chengdu. Within four weeks of our arrival, she had made contact with a doctor in our city.

Though neither we nor the foreign missions committee foresaw it, there was one significant flaw in this plan: our supply of medicine was not long enough to cover the duration of our stay in Dongbei plus the time required to establish new care and resupply the medicine after arriving in Chengdu. While waiting on insurance approval in Chengdu, my wife tried stretching out her remaining doses. Even with this, by the time we had new medicine on-hand – which had to be imported from the United Kingdom – there had been about a month's gap in her treatment. During that gap her body developed an immunity to the drug. It would never work for her again. Our days in China were numbered.

At the time, however, we did not know that the treatment had failed. All we knew was that her symptoms had returned: she was experiencing regular discomfort, and she was beginning to lose weight. Our correspondence from the time indicates that we had some suspicion that her body might have begun to reject the medicine; nevertheless, we held out hope. Perhaps with a bit more time to re-accummulate in and re-permeate her system, the prescription's effectiveness would return?

Yet even as we tried to hold out hope for our personal situation, the general situation in Chengdu began to deteriorate. In the last days of August, a "Declaration for the Sake of the Christian Faith" was published online. This document catalogued official persecution, criticized the Chinese government for instigating the conflict, and professed the church's determination to respect the authorities in secular matters – while refusing all coercion in matters of faith. Within a week, close to three hundred church leaders from across China had added their names. At the top of the list was the name of Pastor Wang Yi of Early Rain Covenant Church in Chengdu. A few days later, I wrote in our weekly letter: "It's hard to think that this will not provoke some sort of significant response; the only real questions are where, when, and to what extent. Some feel that a serious storm may be coming…"

In the two weeks that followed, authorities raided two of Early Rain's church plants in the city. At the same time, the government stepped up pressure on missionaries working with Chinese ethnic minorities. In a single two-week period, the police pressured six families to leave our city – and we heard rumors of related difficulties in neighboring regions. As this continued, my wife began receiving invitations for short-notice "moving sales." We went to a few of these, both to say goodbye and in hopes of providing some "help" by way of purchasing items we really didn't need – but which our neighbors could not take with them and would thus forfeit. The experience is unforgettable: the unwholesome disorder of a life abruptly interrupted, the strange pall that hovers over conversation, and the inescapable feeling that, despite good intentions, one is little better than a vulture. If you have never been in the home of a family on the brink of deportation, be thankful.

As China's National Day (1 October) arrived that year, more bad news struck – and this time much closer to home. "Owen" was a young man we had known ever since arriving in Chengdu. Though not technically part of our team, he worshiped with us on Sunday evenings, regularly participated in our team's events, and taught at the undergraduate college associated with Early Rain. On the Sunday just before National Day, Owen was grabbed by the police while worshiping at Early Rain Covenant Church. Within a few days he had been officially detained and interrogated by both the Public Security Bureau and the Religious Affairs Bureau. Though he was never physically harmed, he was verbally harangued and pressured to implicate Pastor Wang Yi regarding foreign influence. In the end, Owen's visa was cancelled and the authorities gave him a week to leave the country. Before he departed, he and I met for coffee – and I brought him a small Bible that I had carried with me to China whose cover had been bound upside-down.

"I used to say this Bible was a metaphor for my life," I said. "When everything on the outside looks upside-down, everything on the inside is right side-up." Then I gave it to him.

The pressure did not abate. Late that month, I reported the following in one of our letters:

> Yesterday morning, two of my classmates – guys with the same heart as us, and whom I consider to be friends – were missing. Yesterday afternoon, my colleague told me that two of our neighbors were currently being questioned. Last night, a different friend called (via a secure channel) to warn me that nine people in our area of the city had just that day been forced to leave the country...

> This morning when I went to class, one of the two missing classmates had returned. I had a chance to speak to him during our break, and he confirmed what I had half-suspected – that the other missing classmate was one of the nine. He also told me that our neighbor (the one whom I knew was being questioned yesterday) and his family would also likely have to leave. All of these people were part of the same organization, a group particularly focused on minorities – and it appears that the authorities have launched a coordinated move against them nationwide. Late last night we received a report that a family with the same organization in a different province had also been given a week to leave China.

Of course this is but the latest in a steady stream of fireworks we've been seeing all around us. But this is the closest it has come to us. The classmate who is now gone sat right behind me everyday.... I had personally encouraged him to stay in our class when he was experiencing some doubt about whether to drop to a lower level. Now, just like that, he's gone. Similarly, the wife of our neighbor is our children's piano teacher...

It was really something to be there with my remaining classmate as he relayed all this news to me. He has been told that his name is also on the "hit list," and so he and his wife were unable to even try to get to sleep last night until after 2:30 AM. Why 2:30 AM? Because that is when the last flight leaves the Chengdu airport... and they figured that if they made it past that time, there wouldn't be any knocks on their door until at least the morning. He is expecting to be taken in for questioning within the next few days...

I'm supposed to have lunch with this classmate tomorrow (we had arranged last week to meet for lunch to discuss language learning strategies). Now I'm not sure if I'll see him again or not. I'd like to send him a message to see if everything is okay, but we don't have a secure channel between us. So I don't have a good option except to wait and see if he comes to class tomorrow...

In the end, this second friend came to class and we enjoyed a final lunch together. After we finished, I walked him back to his now-disheveled apartment. His wife and daughter had already left the country; he would follow within a day. Not all the leaves had fallen in Chengdu... but the branches were increasingly bare.

Chapter 24:
Dreaming in Chinese

Despite the concerns for my wife's health, and even amidst the gathering clouds of crackdowns in our city, our outlook remained hopeful in autumn 2018. The Lord had brought us through so much already. Surely we would find a way to renew my wife's strength and treatment. And with our family still in the language acqusition phase of missionary life, we suspected that we remained well off the radar of the Chinese authorities. Though we grieved at every deportation, we also believed that we would ride out the current situation and continue. Why else had the Lord brought us here?

In mid-October 2018, my three eldest sons and I took our first camping trip into the mountains of western Sichuan with a group of other expat dads and boys. Upon my return, I wrote a weekly letter that summarizes well the state of my heart and mind in those days:

> I'd like to tell you a tale of two cities. Both of them lie far away from most of you. But for us, both of them are very real – and represent a big part of why we are here.
>
> The first city is Kangding, where the three eldest boys and I traveled last weekend for our camping trip. With a population of only about 100,000, Kangding is tiny

by Chinese standards. What makes it so interesting is that it sits on the ancient border between China and Tibet. About 800 years ago, it was the capital of a kingdom called Chakla – and for centuries it served as an important trading center between its much bigger neighbors. About 300 years ago, however, the Qing dynasty took control of the city. It is now well within the borders of Sichuan province.

Our bus took about six hours to reach Kangding. Upon arrival our group, consisting of eleven boys and four dads, strapped on our packs and hiked about two hours into the mountains. Our campsite was situated at about 9,900 feet above sea level, in a meadow where local black yaks come to water. It may have been the highest anybody in our family has ever hiked, let alone camped – and it was definitely one of the coldest nights I've ever spent outdoors! Nevertheless, we had a great time...

The second city is our own, Chengdu – to which all of us returned safely. On Tuesday night of this week, my second son and I decided to spend our weekly father-son time hanging out on the roof of our building. I smoked my pipe, he ate some shaved ice, and we watched YouTube together. Later that night, however, I returned to the roof alone to look at the city again. With its more than fourteen million people, an ever-expanding urban zone, and undying lights, Chengdu is so much different from Kangding.

However, as I spent time in each city over the past week, I have been haunted by the same thought: who will tell all these people about Jesus? On our way back to the bus as we were leaving Kangding, I walked past the ruins of an old home and was struck by the thought: who had lived in that place? How many significant moments of somebody's life had occurred within those moldering walls... now gone forever? And now that it is becoming more and more difficult for outsiders to live in a place like Kangding, how many more will be lost?

And yet a very similar question can be asked from the rooftop of my own building here in Chengdu. How many millions of stories are being played out all around me every day? And despite all the city lights… how many of those stories have any connection to the only true Light in the universe?

Recently I have been reading a biography of Robert Morrison, the first Protestant missionary to this nation. As I have reflected on his life and work, and as I conferenced this week with a few of my colleagues, it struck me just how similar our current labors remain to Morrison's pioneering work. In both cases – and perhaps in every similar situation – there was/is a threefold objective:

1) Incarnation,
2) Proclamation/Translation, and
3) Perpetuation.

Two hundred years ago, Morrison pursued these objectives through: language learning, translating the Bible, developing language-learning resources, and establishing a college. Nowadays, we do much the same as we learn the language, facilitate resource translation, and assist the local presbytery in its organization and theological education. The continuity is encouraging.

Moreover, it is said that on the day that Robert Morrison embarked from England, a cynic put the question to him quite bluntly: did he really expect to make an impression on the darkness of the great Empire of the East? Morrison is said to have replied, "No, sir. I expect God will!"

In the end, this is what gave Morrison hope to carry on and persevere over almost three decades. It is this which gives me hope. I don't know what will happen in either Kangding or Chengdu. This week a school run by one of the local congregations was raided and threatened, and just today I learned that a nearby coffee shop will be closing because the owner has to leave. What will we see next?

Nevertheless, I still expect that God will make a great impression on this land. When He says, "Let there be light," no darkness can restrain His hand. All the world's history can be refracted through the history of Jesus Himself – especially on that day when His hands were tied to a tree. On that day, the darkness seemed to score an irreversible victory. Yet three days later, the darkest deed ever done proved to be its own undoing as Christ emerged from death in invincible victory. Someday, somehow, the same will happen here – and everywhere else.

Though distance (and pollution) made it impossible to see from my rooftop, our city contained a physical embodiment of my hopes for China: the New Century Global Center. With more than 18 million square feet, it is the world's largest building by floor space. It has hundreds of shops, a glass skybridge on its upper level, and even an indoor waterpark! "Imagine," I said to Rob one day as we were riding an escalator at the Global Center, "if all the industry and resources used to produce this place were focused for the gospel!"

Amidst my rooftop and escalator musings, however, the deportations all around us were taking a serious toll on my wife. Our cross-cultural training had prepared us well for saying goodbye to family and friends prior to leaving America. But it had not warned us just how many goodbyes we should expect to experience as missionaries on the field. As more and more families vanished – including families from within our own *xiǎoqū* – she confided to me that her frustrations and heartache were piling up. She'd even felt some jealousy toward those we knew who had been deported.

This was a shocking turn for her. Just the previous month she had written in her journal:

> I've begun to see our children grow, not just physically, but grow in their faith, and in their view of the vastness of this world. My prayer is that they will continually grow in faith and grow in their love for this country, this city, this people, this culture, ever expanding their hearts and minds to love others as they love themselves, to count others more significant, and to embrace His people as one body. So thankful for my Heavenly Father, who has graciously blessed us and continually cares for us, now, and in the years to come.

How did we seek to work through these hard feelings? My journal records the following:

We had a long conversation the other night, in which I encouraged her to see her calling not simply as "raising the kids," but as "raising the kids amidst the challenges of China." If she holds to the former, she will see the language and lifestyle as barriers to her calling. But if she embraces the latter, then these things – challenging as they truly are – become part of the blessing of her (expanded) calling. "Not barriers, but blessings" must be our motto. Father, help us.

On the day after Thanksgiving, the next entry in my journal struck a more hopeful note:

Psalm 100:1. Imagine the scene: the whole earth, including the animals, trees, and hills, together celebrating the God-ness and goodness of God... a world of love and power and self-control in consummate measure.

For now, we hear the music faintly – and the laughter is but a sweet whisper at the edge of our hope. But it will not always be so. Someday gladness will clothe us in its smooth, shining warmth – and we will dance in the presence of the Lord, full to bursting with the music of eternity. And this will just be the first day of forever...

Chapter 25:
A Year in the Missionary Life

By the end of autumn 2018, our family had passed the one-year mark of our missionary life in China. Between all the major events in this period, there were a lot of ordinary days and weeks. What did our "regular" life look like?

Throughout our time in China, I submitted quarterly reports. These reports went not only to the other ministers in our mission, but also to our home congregation, presbytery, and foreign missions office in the United States. Reviewing these reports for 2018 provides a good picture of our life during our first year in Chengdu. For example, at the end of June my report included the following summary of our family's general life rhythm:

> Our living situation is a blessing. We live in the same apartment complex with Rob and Esther's family, and therefore enjoyed regular fellowship with them this quarter. Our children and their children play regularly, my wife and Esther can go shopping together easily, and Rob and I are able to consult face-to-face on a few minutes' notice over matters related to our work.
>
> Our location is also convenient for the logistics of life. We are close to the international ATM, our Chinese bank,

several fruit stands, a couple of restaurants that we like, and a Walmart. The language school where my wife and the children study is about a fifteen-minute walk, and the university where I study is only about ten minutes further. We are able to get groceries without much hassle, and we are all receiving regular exercise. Our children have also been able to obtain things they enjoy – bicycles, skateboards, LEGO, and digital accessories – with relative ease. They have also found friends among other expat children.

Our Lord's Days this quarter continued as they have since our arrival in Chengdu. In the mornings, we gathered with a handful of other expatriate families for Small Group Church. In the evenings, we gathered in a small rented space with our team colleagues for an evening worship service.

Most weeks followed a predictable pattern, as I reported at the end of the year:

The pattern of our daily life this quarter remained unchanged from previous quarters... I attended language classes four mornings a week at a local university. My family attended classes at private language school three mornings each week. In the afternoons, I continued my studies at home and my wife homeschooled our children. Our eldest son is enrolled in an online Christian high school based in the United States, and our second son attended a math/science co-op taught twice weekly by one of our teammates. On Sunday mornings we attended a home-based, small group church with a handful of other evangelical expat families. On Sunday evenings we attended a team worship service.

As these excerpts indicate, our family devoted a significant portion of time each week to language learning. My classes at the university followed a traditional, textbook-based approach. The daily classes were subdivided into four sections: the first two dedicated to reading and writing, the second two to listening and speaking. At the private school where my family studied and where I received additional tutoring, the teachers employed the Growing Participator Approach. Modeled after the way we acquire our native languages, this approach prioritizes spoken language over written language, with a special emphasis placed upon listening comprehension.

Although our language acquisition never proceeded as fast as we would have liked, over the course of our first year both my wife and I noticed encouraging progress. As my university classes ended in June, I wrote the following in one of our public letters:

> With classes at the university now finished for the semester, I have significant freedom to structure my Chinese studies as I please... my main emphasis this summer is vocabulary acquisition and oral comprehension. To that end, I've added several hundred new words to my "to learn" list, and am practicing not just recognizing them visually (by identifying the Chinese characters), but also recognizing them orally (simply by the sound). The latter is significantly more difficult in Chinese, since many words sound identical – or differ only in their tone. Despite the difficulty, this study strategy has already proven useful.
>
> Another tool I'm using this summer are "graded readers." A graded reader is a storybook, written entirely in Chinese, but which uses an intentionally limited set of vocabulary... In fact, just this morning I finished my first Chinese book – a Chinese abridgement and adaptation of H.G. Wells's *The Country of the Blind*. The text used about 300 distinct characters and a vocabulary of about 400 words. The experience has convinced me of the value of studying in this way... I am hoping to begin creating my own "graded reader" based on the Bible. Starting with Mark's Gospel, I will copy the Chinese text into a Word document. Then, working through it sentence by sentence, I will mark the difficult vocabulary – creating a footnote for each that gives the pronunciation and definition. This project will accomplish several goals: 1) it provides me with a good, structured way to study the Book in Chinese; 2) it creates a resource that can be shared with future language learners; and 3) it will enable me, over time, to create a Chinese version of the Bible that will work on Amazon Kindle – since Word

documents, properly formatted, can easily be converted to Kindle books.

As a busy mother, my wife could never give language study full-time attention. This was her frequent frustration. However, by the end of July she had passed a significant milestone:

> This week in class, my wife completed another book in her curriculum. The book is called *Huli he Muji* (*The Fox and the Hen*). There are not words in this book, only pictures – the story must be narrated in Chinese by the student, with supplement and correction from the teacher. So... when all of you see her again, ask her to tell you the story of the fox and the hen in Mandarin!

Alongside such progress remained plenty of humbling moments. In the same letter in which I recounted my wife's milestone, I added the following:

> One of the great challenges for a Westerner studying Chinese is learning to listen not just to the sounds of words, but also to the tones of the words – since these change the meaning. For example, this week my tutor kept saying to me "yòu shǒu" (right hand). Even though he was waving his right hand at me while saying this, all I could make out was "yǒu shǒu" (have a hand). It was both embarrassing and amusing.

Beyond our primary focus on language learning, our family also found many ways to serve. Some of these we have already mentioned. During my first months in Dongbei, I read through all of our mission's old reports and wrote the first *Brief History of the China Mission*. In Chengdu, I worked on the Chinese church-planting manual, revised bylaws for our mission, and drafted our mission's five-year plan. I served as our team's primary pulpit supply – preaching almost every Sunday evening from behind the coffee shop counter – and as a Sunday School teacher for our mission's teenage boys. I discussed the Bible with my tutor and taught at the Chinese marriage retreat. Additionally, as I was studying the language, I wrote a resource for future language learners: *A Beginner's Guide to Studying Mandarin Chinese*. I served as a sounding board for Rob, reducing the number of calls he had to make to the home office in the United

States. In particular, I helped him navigate some difficult disciplinary cases raging at that time among the pastors in the Huaxi presbytery. Eventually I joined Jack and Rob on the Chengdu team's leadership council.

As for my wife, her primary ministry to our team was managing our household and our children's education – a significantly more challenging task in China than it ever was in Pennsylvania. She also regularly taught Sunday School to the children in our Small Group Church. Beyond this foundational service, my wife had an important ministry by example to our children's tutor, and shared her experience as an educator with prospective Chinese homeschooling parents.

One of the most special ministry experiences ever presented to our family in China occurred two days before Christmas 2018, when the owner of our local Western-themed restaurant – a Christian lady – invited my wife and daughter to come and help her teach a class to Chinese children on making gingerbread houses. Though at first this invitation seemed like a tedious addition to an already exhausting week, my girls accepted. In the end, they were glad they did: as part of the class, my wife was asked to explain to all the children and their parents the meaning of Christmas. In agreeing to help make gingerbread houses, she had received the greatest Christmas gift of all: the chance to share Jesus with those who did not know Him!

Despites its challenges – despite all of our concerns over health and persecution, and despite our frustrations in acquiring the language – our first year as missionaries in China proved to be more fruitful than we had expected. Our lives were incredibly full; fuller than they had ever been! But they were full of good things.

Chapter 26:
The Hammer and the Sickle

By late November, our family spirits had recovered somewhat, thanks to a visit from my in-laws and a second camping trip that I took with my three eldest sons. We camped in a place called *Sìgūniángshān* ("Four Sisters Mountain"). As one might guess, the eponymous mountain has four peaks, one of which rises more than 20,000 feet above sea level – the easternmost mountain of this height in the world. Though unprepared to scale the summit, we camped at more than 10,000 feet – another first in our experience of the wide world.

Likewise, by this time the situation in Chengdu seemed to have stabilized. None of our departed friends had returned; however, we no longer received frequent reports of fresh deportations. For now, the black tide seemed to have receded.

The week before Thanksgiving, Rob and I had lunch with one of the local Huaxi pastors, "Silas." My wife and I had met Silas on our exploratory trip to Chengdu the year prior, and I had occasionally attended worship at his church. Silas was also fluent in English.

We sat down with Silas that day not only to discuss the recent events, but also to ask his advice on how we could best serve the Chinese churches during this season. What would serve them best: for us to make a show of solidarity by openly participating in their worship, or for us to fade into the background in order to lower their and our risk profile? Both Rob and I were willing to pursue the former course; but in this case the reality was that we would probably only get one "strike" with the authorities before we would face deportation. Owen's experience seemed to leave little room for doubt.

As if to underscore the seriousness of all of this: just before leaving to meet Silas, Rob had received a phone call from a local police officer. Our team had had encounters with this particular policeman in the past: he was the same man who had come to my apartment and told Esther that Jack was a "spy." On this occasion, the policeman had asked Rob questions about his family, his source of income, and – strangely enough – whether he planned to leave the country before September 2019. He claimed that this call was part of a routine check-up for all foreigners, but I never received such a call before or after – so we had our suspicions that there was more behind the questioning.

"But we are here to serve you," I remember saying to Silas. "So you tell us what is best. Should we come to worship with you, or stay away?"

Silas's answer was unequivocal. Government surveillance of the Huaxi churches would likely remain heightened for at least another four months, and during that time he advised both Rob and me not to attend public worship at the Huaxi churches. In his judgment, we were long-term investments – and to put our future service at risk in this manner was unnecessary. Besides, there were better ways to serve. Rob had plenty to do for the Huaxi churches behind the scenes at the seminary and in the presbytery. For myself, Silas suggested I might work with one of their bilingual homegroups or perhaps coach some of their bilingual church planters. In this manner I could be of service to the church, while at the same time using as much Mandarin as possible. It seemed like a wise plan.

Then came 9 December 2018.

While Rob and his family were away in Shanghai for a meeting of representatives from various Chinese presbyteries, the government dropped the hammer and the sickle on Early Rain Covenant Church. In an urgent prayer letter sent the next day, I wrote:

This is an urgent call for you to pray for the church here in our city – upon whom, beginning yesterday evening, the authorities have launched a large-scale attack. Thus far, somewhere between 50-80 people have been arrested, with arrests continuing through last night into today. Policemen have come to people's homes in the middle of the night, knocked down doors, used searchlights, and either arrested or made threats – including threatening parents for not sending their children to government schools. There are reports that even some children have been arrested with their parents by the authorities. This is a widescale, coordinated attack involving several departments from multiple levels of the government.

The building where Early Rain Covenant Church meets is now under total police lockdown. The undergraduate college, the seminary and library, and even one of the library's offsite storage facilities have been raided. Although initially centered on Early Rain Covenant, the attack now seems to be spreading outward to the leaders and members of other Huaxi congregations and church plants.

So far, everybody from our team is safe and have not had any contact with the authorities or police. In God's plan, my closest colleague and his family were out of town this weekend – which may have helped shield them. We remain very concerned for their safety. I have been to his home twice now to check for police notices or signs of forced entry. So far, all looks clear. Ask God to keep it so!

Three days later, we sent the following update:

The arrests that began on Sunday night continued into last night. The strategy of the authorities seems to be to track down every single person belonging to Early Rain Covenant Church. Some persons, when found, are simply arrested. With others, the police try to force them to sign a pledge never to return to the church – or pressure members of their family to make them sign. Many who refuse to sign have been arrested. Some have been released but remain under constant surveillance. The whereabouts and welfare of others remain unknown.

It's hard to keep track of everything that's happened, but according to a friend who is in direct contact with many, the sufferings now borne by those connected to this church include "being systematically hunted down, imprisoned, beaten, stripped naked, robbed, driven from their homes, pressured by their employers, deported to hometowns, sent to reeducation centers, and more." Last evening, many small groups took courage and met together. They knew full well what this could mean, and indeed police came to at least one of these groups. From this group only two escaped; everybody else was arrested.

Some news is now trickling out regarding those who are being detained. The church's main leader, his wife, two of the elders, and at least one sister are being held pending formal charges being filed against them. In addition, around 50 students from the undergraduate college or the seminary remain in custody; it seems that the plan is to send them each back to their hometowns (where you can be sure the local police will be waiting). In the meantime, they have persuaded those who are detaining them to allow them to read the Bible and sing together each day.

We remain concerned about the security of my closest colleague, who worked closely with at least one of those who are awaiting formal charges. With the higher levels of the government now involved, it's hard to say whether his identity may yet be discovered through technology. And with the lower levels of the government now resorting to abusive force in the treatment of the church, it is impossible to know what sort of information could be revealed under duress. Please ask God to continue protecting my colleague, his family, and his place here.

As for my family, we have very little reason to suspect that we will attract any attention. In fact, this week I received the papers from my university which give me the green light to reapply for visas. This was a kind mercy from God – a beam of sunlight in the midst of the surrounding gloom.

Yet it is a bit surreal to be going about our daily life when we know that so many of our brothers and sisters are suffering. Imagine what it must be like to go to class and play the role of the cheerful student – when mere miles away, one knows that men and women to whom one is eternally bound in Christ are being hunted like animals and arrested! One feels rather like Fredegar "Fatty" Bolger from *The Lord of the Rings* – the one hobbit who stayed behind in the Shire to maintain Frodo's cover story while Frodo, Sam, Merry, and Pippin rode off to face the Shadow.

The attack on Early Rain Covenant Church created shockwaves among churches all across China. Although not entirely unforeseen, the draconian aggression and persistent malice evident in the government response garnered international media attention. Detailed reports appeared not only in Christian periodicals like *WORLD*, but also in secular publications such as *The New York Times*.

Five days after the attack on Early Rain, Rob and his family returned safely from Shanghai to Chengdu. This was a tremendous answer to prayer, for we were all concerned that he might be detained at the airport. Our family breathed a major sigh of relief, for it seemed that the Lord had at least spared us our greatest fear. The attack on Early Rain had made it clear that Jack and his family could not return to China, given Jack's connections to Wang Yi. If Rob and Esther were forced to leave China, our family would have felt marooned.

Two days after Rob and Esther safely returned to Chengdu, I was walking my family to their Chinese classes when Rob called. One does not need much imagination to guess at the outcome of the conversation that followed. Three nights later, I accompanied Rob and Esther and their kids to the airport. The next morning, our weekly letter began as follows:

This has been the hardest week of our life in China.

The authorities continue to ravage the local church. At least fifteen of the leaders and staff connected to Early Rain and its schools remain in jail. Today about a half dozen moving trucks were seen in front of the church building. All of the physical resources belonging to the church, the seminary, the library, and the bookstore – everything is gone. Police continue to seek, harass, and threaten the church... We have received credible information suggesting that, so far from receding, the storm will continue to spread for at least the next six months.

In the shadow of all this, on Monday my closest colleague and I made the difficult decision that he and his family needed to return to North America. His involvement with the local church, especially with the seminary and its library, along with his links to several who are now in jail, made it seem to us more and more likely that he would be confronted. Such a situation would not only inhibit his future labors here, but also bring greater pain upon the local church. This latter point was the most relevant to us – as we have come to serve, not to harm.

When we first came to this city, our team consisted of 19 others: 10 adults and 9 children. As of this morning, only 2 adults of those original 19 remain. Not all were deported, of course: one family relocated, and another couple realigned with a different team. Nevertheless... there will be far fewer faces at Christmas.

The loss of my closest colleague and his family is a particularly difficult blow for our family. Their kids have been my children's best friends here in China, and Rob and Esther have been our closest neighbors and friends since we arrived. It's just baffling to think that they are now gone. It's even more startling when we consider that this was God's premeditated plan: all along it was His intention to bring us here, make us happy, and then leave us bereaved. It's an awful thought – both in the historical ("full of awe") and contemporary ("difficult to accept") sense.

In a private letter written to Jack the day Rob and Esther left, the picture was more raw:

> For me, the primary emotion right now is just bafflement – because I cannot imagine yet what the Lord intends to do with and in us through this. But my wife is far more aggrieved. She's been going through some of the usual

stages of grief: denial, anger, and apathy. I asked her last night if Rob and Esther's departure made her want to leave China, and she said, "Yes." Today after returning successfully from the visa office, I said, "Good news about the visas, huh?" When she made an ambivalent expression, I asked her, "Were you hoping they'd be denied?" She sort of shrugged and said, "It wouldn't be the worst thing. This just confirms our marooned-ness."

...We know that our local brothers and sisters are suffering far worse depredations right now, and we know that Rob and Esther are also suffering. But we too are hurting in this, and these events raise some pretty big questions about our future. I'm trying to advise everybody – Rob, Esther, my wife, and myself – that people in shock don't make good decisions, and so we should all be very cautious about making any long-term decisions. But it's hard for all of us not to feel gloomy...

Yet despite the pain, we endeavored to retain theological perspective and servants' hearts. Our public letter from the week of Rob and Esther's departure concluded with these words:

This morning, as I prepared for my Sunday evening message to our team, I was struck by the number of parallels from the first Christmas to our experience this week. If you look in the second chapter of Matthew's Gospel, you'll see what I mean: a ravaging government, a family that had to flee ahead of the sword, and the suffering of many who could not escape. So many jagged edges.

In the midst of all this, duty continued. On Wednesday I achieved high marks in my final exam for the semester. On Thursday I successfully applied for our family's visa extensions... But in the aftermath of our friends' departure, such victories do not taste as sweet. Indeed, we have been tempted in a much less thankful direction...

Our souls are tired from carrying such heavy hearts. There's no question that Jesus is worth all of it. Nor do we disbelieve the promise that "all things work together for good." As many of you know, I have a relatively well-developed imagination – but even for me it is difficult to imagine what God intends to do through these things.

Keep praying for the sufferings of the local church. Pray for my colleague and his family as they return to North America and try to process all that's happened. And please also pray for those of us who remain.

Summarizing all of this, my only private journal entry for the period recorded these words:

Fire has a wonderful way of focusing the mind. A fire in the home will seize one's attention away from all other meditations or occupations, be they ever so valuable. Fire does not long bear being ignored.

Fire has engulfed the church in our city. The sufferings of the saints are terrible, tragic, and unrelenting. My closest colleague here and his family have had to leave China. Like the Christmas in Matthew 2, ours features terror, flight, and suffering.

This makes our future uncertain in several ways. It does not, however, change our calling or our focus in the near term. We are to live here, alone if need be, to learn the language and culture of these beloved and benighted people. Lord, hold us steady.

Chapter 27:
The Fellowship of the Cross

There is nothing quite like cross-cultural isolation to teach you the true value of friendship. In your home culture where relationships are much easier to make, break, and replace, it is all too easy to take them for granted. In a foreign culture, however, every familiar face counts. You smile more broadly when you see them. And when they vanish, you miss them more fiercely...

With our team shattered and our national partners under surveillance, our sense of being "marooned" – both in terms of fellowship and usefulness – deepened dolefully. I was determined to hunker down, plow ahead in learning Mandarin, and await a brighter dawn. But this was not so easy for my wife – who was now suffering not just from increasing symptoms of her disease, but also from deep pangs of grief and profound uncertainty about our future. As I shared in a private letter to Jack:

> We had such high hopes for Chengdu. And when we first arrived, there were 19 others on our team besides ourselves... After tonight, there will be just two single sisters remaining – both of whom also have plans to leave. In addition to this, we know of many others who have had to leave – and with our contacts in the local

church now under surveillance, there is little hope of much interaction with them for the foreseeable future. This point isn't lost on my wife, either: "Even if you were fluent in Chinese, what could you do here now?" she asked me.

On Christmas Day, we hosted our two remaining teammates for dinner. Although this was sweet fellowship with dear sisters, the harder underlying realities for our family were not getting easier. That same day, I wrote the following in a letter to an old seminary friend:

> The recent departure of Rob and Esther has been very difficult, especially for my wife. Her health also continues to be poor, and this has contributed to hard feelings toward our present situation and the prospect of our future here. She has had a real struggle against a desire to leave.
>
> Ask God to help me be a good husband to her through this time. I'm such an engineer. When a problem arises, I want to deal with it as quickly as possible and move on. I keep my emotions on a short leash, and I can – unless very careful – be impatient with those who seem to be wallowing rather than striving forward. I don't want to leave, and I don't think we are called to leave… and so I want her to stop feeling this way. But I need to be careful in how I talk to her about this, so that she doesn't simply acquiesce out of a desire to avoid upsetting me.

As our marriage and family wrestled through these jarring adjustments, the Lord sent us open hearts and hands. Despite being warned by one North American contact that our associations made us "radioactive," Nathaniel and Verity invited our family to return to Yunnan for the New Year holiday. And in Chengdu, another family from our Small Group Church – "Aquila" and "Priscilla" – made a special point to draw nearer to us rather than to cast us off. The Saturday after Rob and Esther left, Aquila and Priscilla spent several hours talking with us over coffee – then took our whole family out to eat noodles. Without these two couples, we don't know how we could have endured.

Aquila and I became especially good friends during this period. Though he was busy with his own labors and was exposing himself to possible risk by association, Aquila made it a point that we should get together weekly to chat over coffee – or sometimes *jiǎozi*. Despite coming from different places in the world, we found we had much in common – including, of all things, an appreciation for vegemite.

On Aquila's advice, we accepted Nathaniel and Verity's invitation to get out of Chengdu and spend New Year with them in Yunnan. We rang in the New Year together by singing Psalm 90, and over the next few days the change of scenery and the opportunity for conversation with our friends – who had also experienced some recent, painful goodbyes – allowed all of us a bit of an emotional and spiritual "reset." Our first weekly letter for 2019 included the following reflection:

> For us, 2018 was the first calendar year spent entirely in China. It was the year we arrived in Chengdu, and therefore our first year living in a global metropolis. It was the first year of focused language study, and our first year working with our new team. As you all know by now, it was also the year in which the authorities awoke from a long, ambivalent slumber to rain renewed malice upon the church and God's work. Consequently, 2018 became a year full of pleasant hellos, painful goodbyes, and perplexing changes – a year in which God has been teaching us and others to love Him not just for His gifts, but simply for Himself.

The weeks following our return from Yunnan became a blur of activity – and hospitality. In early January, a young seminary couple from California who were considering missions came to visit Chengdu. Being now the "senior" (only) member of our team's leadership council remaining in the city, I had the privilege and responsibility to show them around. Thankfully, the young man had spent a few years living in China prior to seminary, and his Chinese was better than mine – a fact for which we were grateful when it came to registering their arrival with the local police.

In mid-January, my parents arrived for their first-ever visit to China. Our family had been looking forward to this, and the event did not disappoint the expectation. My daughter taught my father to count to ten in Mandarin, and my mother "enjoyed" some harrowing experiences crossing the city streets and riding in taxis. At one point during their stay, I took my parents and my eldest son to see Xi'an and its trio of important sites: the Nestorian Stone, the Terracotta Army, and the ancient city wall. My folks had never experienced anything like it. We even hitchhiked back to the city from the Terracotta Army! Once back in Chengdu, I took my coffee-loving parents to a newly opened shop – where my dad played a sort of duet with the overjoyed *lǎobǎn*. I say "sort of" because my father was playing "Amazing Grace" on the piano, and the shopkeeper on his violin – who didn't know the hymn – tried at first to improvise, then gave up and switched to "Auld Lang Syne."

Ten days after my parents' return to the States, another friend – a former teammate from Dongbei – arrived to celebrate Chinese New Year with us. "Mary" is one of the most adventurous people we've ever met, and with her in town we had quite a few adventures. We braved crowded public sites on Lunar New Year itself. We jumped on county buses to visit a far-flung historic village – the most densely packed place we have ever experienced, even in China. While there, we even added a new entry to our "adventure eating" catalogue: fried black scorpion! For those curious: it tastes something like overcooked, hairy bacon.

As welcome as were all of these visits from family and friends, there was also a downside: every happy greeting inevitably ended with a sorry farewell. For my wife, who was still struggling to process the dissolution of our Chengdu team, these were especially keen. Nevertheless, her journal for early February shows that she was endeavoring to endure:

> My prayer during these lonely times, as I have been reading in a biography about others going through hard times, is that Christ has saved the best wine for last. We may be suffering in other ways, whether outwardly or inwardly, but He uses it for our good, for our sanctification, and ultimately for His glory.

> I am thankful to be a part of His story, wherever He calls me. Lord, help me to remember this in times of cloudiness and in times of sunshine.

Yet while her spirit was rising heavenward, her health was deteriorating further. The day my parents left, I wrote in a private letter to an old friend:

> We had a long and pleasant visit with them... The aftermath, however, is hard. Twice since I got home from the airport, my wife has been in tears. As much as she enjoys these visits (her parents last fall, then mine this month), I think they remind her of everything that we don't have here: extended family, a stable network of friends, and a solid church to anchor our weekly life.

> On top of the emotional struggle, it's also a fact that her health is not great. Although we have a relatively stable supply chain for her medicine, the medicine no longer appears to be working. She suffers from chronic symptoms... Not only has this caused her to lose a noticeable amount of weight, it also affects her quality of life in other ways. For example, at the end of the day when our kids are all "put away for the night" and she wants to relax, the drop in her overall tension levels usually triggers her symptoms. She doesn't complain about it, but it's not easy.

As the Lunar New Year passed, the date approached for us to host the whole-mission retreat for our denominational colleagues in Chengdu. Rob and Esther would not be returning for it, of course, but – after some discussion – we decided that Bruce and his wife, along with Chip and his family, should still come. Though the security situation in Chengdu was tense, we doubted that those of us who remained were under any direct surveillance. Moreover, if ever there was a time that we needed one another's presence, this was it.

And so it was that I found myself on the metro on the Monday night before Valentine's Day, heading toward the airport to pick up Chip and his family. I was about two stops from the airport when I got a secure message from Chip...

They had been in Taiwan visiting with family for the Lunar holiday, but had boarded a plane earlier that day to return to the mainland. When their plane landed in Guangzhou, where they intended to transfer onto a flight to Chengdu, the authorities stopped them in customs. Chip and his wife were informed that they had transgressed China's national security, and could never again enter China. They were put on the next available flight back to Taipei... Chip had messaged me as soon as he could.

Chapter 28:
The Wake-Up Call

Chip and his family... deported.

Stunned, I did the only thing I could think to do. I got off the metro at the next stop, walked across the platform, and got on the next train back toward my home. Now what?

That night was the only time in my life when I have felt truly afraid to go home – but not because I was afraid the police would be waiting. Rather, I feared what the news would do to my wife. Something had changed with her the day we evacuated Rob and Esther; I sensed that her capacity for stress had already reached its limit.

I got off the metro a few blocks from our home and began the winding walk through the local Tibetan flea market. It was after hours: the booths were empty, the shops closed, and the streets dark. I asked the Lord for wisdom and for help... how could I break this news?

As it turned out, my wife took the news better than I expected. She grieved for Chip and his family, of course, but she had never yet met them – and so the blow did not land as heavy as I had feared.

Nevertheless, what were we to do about the retreat? Rob was gone, Chip was gone... was it still safe or wise for Bruce and his wife to come? A few hours of shocked consultation quickly ensued. Though Chip's deportation had blindsided all of us, there were some plausible reasons to believe that it was disconnected from events in Chengdu. The timing was horrible, but the event was perhaps not as portentous as it seemed. In the end, we decided that Bruce and his wife should still attempt to come to Chengdu.

Bruce and "Sue" landed the next day without difficulty. None of us could pretend the "retreat" was as it should be. Nevertheless, we enjoyed our time together. Bruce and I had not always seen eye to eye; but as we got to spend more time together face to face, the tensions eased – and he shared with me some real wisdom about missionary longevity.

The morning after Bruce and Sue arrived, however, I received a call from my father that rattled me to my core.

Communication with my father was not an unusual thing – not even from the far side of the world. We kept in regular communication with my parents via email, Skype, and secure messaging. But to my knowledge, prior to that day, I had received only one "cold call" from my dad – the night my grandmother died.

Unfortunately, the news with this second call was even worse: the wife of one of my ministerial colleagues from Pennsylvania – a man with whom I had been close – had died suddenly and unexpectedly earlier in the week. The cause of death was still uncertain, but there had been no foul play. As far as Dad knew, my friend's wife had been going about her regular motherly duties one night... and the next thing before anybody knew, she was gone.

This was bitter news for both my wife and me: we had fond memories of spending time together with my friend and his wife in Pennsylvania. But for me, the news was beyond incredible; it was convicting. All of a sudden, I was wide awake to the horrifying prospect of my own wife's deteriorating health. For some time, her medicine had been clearly failing and her weight noticeably dropping. To this point, we had simply hoped and prayed that things would get better. But now I wanted to know: how much weight had she lost?

I think it was the same day of my dad's call that I called my wife and asked her to step on our bathroom scale. Then, pulling her health check records from our files, we compared the results: in the year since we arrived in Chengdu, she had lost about thirty pounds! The situation was more serious than either of us had realized.

In the days that followed, I began to ponder our options. My wife was very ill and needed medical intervention. Chip could no longer fulfill the ministry for which he had been called by our denomination. Rob and Jack were gone from Chengdu, and might never return. Bruce would need a new partner, but our family did not wish to return to Dongbei. Where did all this leave us?

Four days after Chip's deportation, I wrote the following to Barnabas:

> As you know, my wife has not been well. Physically, her illness is not responding to the treatment we have currently at our disposal. Emotionally, she has been deeply hurting since Rob and Esther's evacuation. More than once she has asked me: if we were sent here to work with Rob and Jack, and those families cannot be here, what purpose is there to us remaining?
>
> At the same time, it appears that our mission may be facing a workload and resource crunch. Bruce will want a new partner. Chip will want new work – and he has indicated that he is interested in the sort of work, alongside Rob, that was originally envisioned for me.
>
> Our family is not interested in returning to Dongbei... I'm writing because I think there may be a third option. This is painful for me to articulate... but I think I owe it to both my wife and to the rest of the mission to put it before you.
>
> If our family were to leave the field, would it be possible for Chip's family to stay with the mission? Could Chip take up the labors that were intended for me – labors which can serve the Mainland without requiring one to live on the Mainland? Chip is already fluent in Chinese, and because his wife is Taiwanese he can live in Taiwan without the need for a "visa job" – giving his full time to the work of our Mainland mission. At the same time, if Chip's family were to replace us, there would still be resources to provide a new partner for Bruce.

This is hard for me to write, Barnabas, because I love the life the Lord has given my family in Chengdu. I love studying Chinese, I enjoy the culture, and I would greatly enjoy spending the rest of my years serving the global church. But I also recognize that my wife is not well, and that recent events have put our mission in an unforeseen bind. I suppose it comes down to this: if sacrificing my position can help provide a position for Chip, then it's something I'm willing to very seriously consider. Part of me would die in so doing – but living for Christ's kingdom means dying to our personal desires.

A few days after sending this letter, my wife and I had a video call with Barnabas. While he appreciated our concern for Chip and for the greater work of the mission, he did not desire to see us resign. He encouraged us to make my wife's health a priority, "whatever it takes," but also expressed the hope that we could persevere in China – "if you are able."

For the next two months, we took Barnabas's words to heart. Even amidst the flurry of welcoming new teammates to Chengdu – a family from Jack's organization whose plans to come had not been superceded by the events of December – we redoubled our efforts to address my wife's medical situation. She consulted international doctors, Chinese specialists, and eventually underwent an analytical procedure at the local Chinese hospital.

The procedure's conclusion confirmed medically what we already knew experientially: her underlying condition was in full flare. There could be only one cause: the medicine that we and many others had labored so hard to procure had failed. She needed a new treatment.

We formulated a plan. Thanks to the generous support of my wife's parents, we had already been hoping to surprise our children with three weeks of vacation in Pennsylvania during the upcoming summer. If the foreign missions committee would agree to grant us a three-week medical leave of absence in conjunction with that vacation, we could use the extra time to consult with my wife's original specialist about a new path forward. The committee agreed, and we set our departure date for the third week of June.

Yet as we waited, my wife's weight loss seemed to accelerate. As it did, her fatigue and pain increased. Though we were receiving good news about potential new treatments, the possibility of her losing even more weight before getting help was alarming. By mid-May, her total weight loss was approaching fifty pounds.

Hearing this, Barnabas made a suggestion that may well have saved my wife's life. A day after receiving the latest update on her health, he wrote the following: "We'll keep praying. A difficult question for you: are you and your wife really comfortable with waiting another month before returning to the States to start treatment?" That same day, writing from Dongbei, Bruce concurred: "A very good question, Barnabas."

With both Barnabas and Bruce suggesting that we leave as soon as practicable, we decided to try. My wife contacted her doctor in Pennsylvania about moving up her appointment. I spoke to my university about a medical absence and looked into changing our airline tickets. The Lord gave us favor on all sides. We had a plan.

Despite the lengthening shadow of this medical crisis, our last month in China was remarkably positive. My wife and I celebrated our wedding anniversary with an overnight trip to some hot springs in the nearby mountains – a trip that she described as "perfect." Then, two days before our departure, I successfully passed HSK 4 – a standard examination for foreigners studying Chinese. As we boarded our flight, everything seemed to be moving in the right direction: we were leaving China for a season, but we would return stronger.

Chapter 29:
Hard Realities

Our first days back in Pennsylvania were full of amusing moments of reverse culture shock. At a restaurant with my in-laws, one of my boys pointed to the other customers and said to me, "Look, *Bàba* – *wàiguórén!*" After dinner, we went to a supermarket – and my wife and I were both a bit overwhelmed by the selection. There were whole aisles devoted to beer, cereal, and cheese!

Things became far less amusing, however, when we met with my wife's specialist the following week. His explanation of the failure of her current medicine was simple: with that type of drug, any gap in treatment allows the body to build up a tolerance and effectively ruins the treatment thereafter. This was the bad news. The good news, however, was that there was one more drug that would almost certainly work for her. But this second drug had some hard strings attached. First, it would take about sixteen weeks to get her properly inducted on the medication. Second – and far more critically in terms of managing her disease – she must not miss a scheduled treatment. Stopping these types of drugs is not only dangerous, it would allow the body to build up an immunity.

We left the specialist's office feeling both encouraged and conflicted. On the one hand, it was such a relief to have an explanation of the first medicine's failure and a concrete plan for the future. On the other hand, it only took one glance at the calendar to know that a sixteen-week induction period would push our return to China back further than we expected. But most troubling of all was the doctor's warning about missing a scheduled treatment. As far as we knew, this new proposed drug was the only other drug available to manage my wife's illness. What if we returned to China and ran into logistic problems with the drug? This was a very real possibility, as the drug would need to be imported.

Beyond these major concerns, we also faced a cluster of secondary considerations. Our international doctors in Chengdu were general practitioners. They had expressed some willingness to administer the medication, provided it could be obtained. However, they were advising that my wife would need to see a specialist annually – either in Hong Kong or in Thailand. Although not impossible in principle, this would create some cascading issues for our family in terms of childcare, education, etc. It would also add considerably to the cost of our missionary support package.

The next day, I boarded a train to New York City to visit an old friend. For almost the entirety of my trip there and back, I was praying and thinking how to balance two factors. The first was my first responsibility to care for my family (1 Tim. 5:8). The second was our responsibility to honor the investment made by so many to prepare, send, and support our family's missionary labors in China. To go back to China before my wife was fully recovered seemed to violate the former. But to resign from missionary service seemed to violate the latter. Stuck between these options, I was simply at a loss to know how to proceed. But finally, after returning home from New York and talking further with my wife, I realized that there might be a third way. The next day I wrote the following to Jack:

> There are two principles that lie at the core of our thinking. The first is that we are not ready to pull the plug on ministry to the Chinese. The second is that we do not believe it is wise to return to China until my wife's health, both physical and emotional, is significantly recovered.

Where that leaves us is this: we are proposing that we leave Chengdu and remain in Pennsylvania for the next year. During that time, my wife can be under consistent care and treatment from her current specialist. For my part, I can continue studying Chinese – using the resources I have on-hand, and also trying to take advantage of the Mandarin-speaking community (including a Chinese church) in the university city. By next summer, we should have a better idea of whether her health can be sustained overseas. We would also have a better idea of where both you and Rob are going to settle. The denomination is probably going to want my family and Rob's to be reunited. Thus if we are able to return to Asia next year, we could simply plan to follow them – whether that is to the Mainland or to Taiwan.

I am very concerned about what a premature return to Chengdu could do to my wife's health. Her weight is down severely... and even if the new medicine works wonders it will take time for her to get to a healthy place. Moreover, I am concerned about the integrity of medicine imported into China. We have friends who ordered medication through the international doctors in Chengdu – only to find out later that what the supplier had sold the doctors was fake. If that happened even once to my wife on the new medicine, her body could become immune – putting her at very serious risk again. China simply isn't a place to experiment with her health. We cannot go back until we know she is recovered, stable, and sustainable.

In addition to this physical issue, I am concerned about her emotional and spiritual health. She's never quite gotten over the fact that your family and Rob's family had to leave, and she told me last night that she's "never really felt like a missionary." She realizes that her illness and the constant fatigue is affecting her judgment; nevertheless in her current condition she isn't able to serve joyfully. The spirit is willing, but the flesh is weak.

Although he had some misgivings about our proposal, Jack agreed. So did Rob and Bruce. With their blessing, a few days later I sent the proposal to Barnabas and James – and we made an appointment to speak the following week. It seemed like we had found a way.

Two nights before my scheduled call, my wife and I had another long conversation. Though she was willing to defer to me and to the foreign missions committee, she confessed that she did not wish to live in limbo for a whole year before getting some closure on whether we would be returning to China. Therefore, she hoped that Barnabas and James would encourage me to resign. With this in mind, the following day I wrote to Barnabas:

> Since I know that we may be discussing a difficult decision tomorrow morning, I thought I'd write to you this morning with an update that might help. This won't be brief, but I wanted to help you be as informed as possible before we speak. (And of course you may feel free to share this with James.)
>
> First, I'm attaching a letter from my wife's doctor in Chengdu (written at our request), recommending that we spend a year outside of China and explaining some of the difficulties that will be involved in managing her care long-term. I send this to you for two reasons: a) so that, if needed, it can be shared with the Committee; and b) because I think it illustrates the realities we will face in managing her health long-term.
>
> Because of these realities, I think it's unrealistic and unwise for us to plan on returning to the Mainland, now or in the future. If the Committee decides to send Rob and his family to Taiwan, that could be a possibility for us as well — Taiwan has world-class healthcare. But I don't presume upon the Committee's plans, and I know we are leery in our denomination about letting circumstances dictate plans.
>
> Second, although we are willing to wait for a year before making a final decision if the Committee so desires, I think I should share with you that my wife is hoping that you and James will recommend that the Committee encourage us to seek a new call. I think she just feels spent. And while it's likely that her overall spirits will improve over the next year, I cannot guarantee that this

will translate into a desire to go back to Asia – even to Taiwan.

For this reason, although we want the Committee to make the decision, and although I would love the opportunity to spend the next year continuing my Chinese studies, I'm not sure I can guarantee that it would make a difference.

Third, I want to express to you that serving in China has been one of the greatest privileges of my ministry – despite being at the same time the most difficult. The Lord has changed us for the better through these 20 months. Though I do not regard myself as having made a good return on the Committee's investment, both my wife and I are so thankful for the Committee's entrusting us with this opportunity. Though it also seems to us that the door for residential service is now closing, our heart for the Chinese and global church remains wide open. I'm not sure if we can ever again live abroad, and I think we are going to have to try to find some stability for our kids (who have proven to be quite adaptable, but are also facing a lot of changes in a short time); but if there are ways that I can honor this and still be of service, please do inform me.

Though it would be another day until we spoke, it seemed to me as I sent this email that the conclusion was all but foregone. We had given our lives to China...

...but we would not be going back.

Chapter 30:
Farewell to the Middle Kingdom

Despite the suffering of the saints and the trials we faced, I had loved our life in Chengdu. It was harder than anything we had previously experienced, yet amidst the hardship there was also a joy to life in the Middle Kingdom. As I wrote in my private journal:

> Every street full of color and faces is like an animated, living library – a moving, colorful collection of human stories, with pages turning toward eternity. What a beautiful privilege it is to be here and learn these stories. What an opportunity it would be to help even a small fraction find a happy ending that lasts forever.

Before we left Pennsylvania, the most delightful scene my heart could imagine in this world was a leaf-strewn path in an autumn wood. Before we left Chengdu, however, a new image had come alongside this old memory:

> About two blocks from our home, down by the river, there is a waterfront area that has been deliberately reconstructed to resemble "old Chengdu." It's about a half-kilometer in length, and in this place both sides of the river are lined with canopies, tables, and tea-houses. During the day, many retired folks come to this area to

drink tea, play games, and talk. For less than 1 USD, you can buy a jug of green tea... and then sit for hours. The combination of the river and the conversation makes just enough background chatter, and there is a wonderful ambiance of tobacco smoke... it's perfect there.

We had lived in China for less than two years. But China now lived in our hearts.

Nevertheless, when I spoke with Barnabas and James that Thursday morning in June, there was unanimity in our judgment: the Lord was calling our family to leave China and seek a new call. Having come to this conclusion, we chatted briefly about arrangements: the foreign missions committee was prepared to be generous to help us make a smooth transition back to the States, and they would cover the cost of tickets so that myself, my wife, and two of our sons could briefly return to Chengdu in August. With these assurances and their encouragement, that same day I submitted the following letter of resignation:

Dear Members of the Foreign Missions Committee –

"The LORD gave, and the LORD has taken away;
blessed be the name of the LORD."

赏赐的是耶和华，收取的也是耶和华。
耶和华的名是应当称颂的。

I write to you today with thanksgiving in my heart, both to the Lord Jesus and to this Committee, for the extraordinary privilege of serving as an evangelist to China for nearly two years. Although the last 20 months have been the most difficult of my ministry, they have also been among the most rewarding. Though I do not regard my contribution to the work in China, nor my return on the Committee's investment, as particularly significant, nevertheless both my wife and I are grateful to you men, and to the whole denomination, for entrusting us with this privilege. Through our time in China, the Lord has changed us and our children for the better.

However, the Lord has also challenged us with serious health concerns, particularly regarding my wife. When we left China in late May, we hoped that these concerns might be relatively simple to resolve. I sincerely expected that our family would be returning to China in early August. In retrospect, my expectation now seems to me to have been almost irrationally optimistic. Indeed, as subsequent medical consultation has demonstrated, the treatment of my wife's disease and her physical recovery will be a long road. Even now that we have a plan, there remains much uncertainty – though we are comforted that our God is certain!

In addition to physical depletion due to her disease, my wife has suffered immense emotional and spiritual stress due to the extraordinary situation that has developed in China over the past eight months. As persecution and eviction of foreign missionaries has erupted on a scale unseen for decades, our access to the Chinese church has been effectively cut off – and we were personally involved in evacuating the primary colleagues with whom we were sent to co-labor. The ensuing grief, isolation, and elevated stress have taken their toll on all of us – but especially on my wife. She is not presently able to serve joyfully on the foreign mission field, and I cannot guarantee that she will ever again feel so inclined. We all have our capacity for change, stress, and uncertainty (three adjectives that apply superlatively to life in China), and I believe that my wife has reached her capacity for life abroad – at least for this period of our lives.

Having laid all this before the leadership in the days since our return to Pennsylvania, this morning I received their unanimous encouragement to consider this nexus of events as our Father's way of leading my family toward a different future – a future away from China. I am thankful for this counsel, as it was our conviction that the final decision about our continuation with the Committee should rest not with ourselves, but with those who sent us. I want to note particularly how thankful I am for the way the leadership affirmed the Committee's respect for our family's life and labors abroad. Despite my ongoing efforts to dissuade her, my wife has struggled with a sense of guilt over these events – and it helped her greatly to receive such affirmation.

Though I love China, I love my wife more. She is the real hero of our missionary story. The need to care for her physically, emotionally, and spiritually takes priority over, and indeed is a prerequisite for, any ministry I hope to accomplish – whether in China, in North America, or in any corner of the wide world. Therefore, per the recommendation of the leadership, I am writing to the Committee today to tender my resignation as an Evangelist to China – effective 31 July 2019.

Though it seems to us that the door for full-time, residential foreign missionary service has now closed, our heart for the Chinese and global church remains wide open. I cannot say that we will ever again be able to live abroad. Moreover, for the sake of our children – who have proven quite adaptable, but are also facing a lot of unexpected changes in a short time – I think that we are going to have to try to find some sort of stable settlement for the foreseeable future. Yet if there are ways that I can honor this and still be of service, please do not hesitate to contact me.

Yours in the love of Christ for the nations…

Our farewell journey to the Middle Kingdom went without incident – *yílù píng'ān* ("peace on every road"), as the Chinese would say. Nathaniel and Verity came to help us pack. Peter helped us ship boxes. We took our boys to see the Great Wall. And when the moment finally came for us to go to the airport, Aquila turned up to see us off…

Chapter 31:
The School of Christ in the Land of China

Despite being close to persecution geographically, our family never faced a direct physical threat. Like any foreigners living in China, we had our share of regular encounters with various levels of government for things such as police registration, visa renewal, etc. But most of these interactions were strictly routine – or at least as "routine" as such things can be in a nation whose bureaucratic culture predates the birth of Christ. To the best of our knowledge, our missionary activities and connections never attracted sufficient attention to place us on the radar of the Chinese authorities.

Moreover, ordinary Chinese people always treated us with an extraordinary degree of kindness and patience. They were gracious with our fumbling Mandarin, kindly toward our children, and generally did everything they could to help our large family live in their country. Indeed, despite tension between our governments, we believe that we received more grace in China than a Chinese family could generally expect to receive in America.

We love China and its people: their ancient and colorful culture, their enterprising pragmatism, their patient resilience – and yes, even their difficult language. The image of China too often depicted in our popular media is characterized by

Western assumptions and priorities; it is as inaccurate as it is unhelpful. The Chinese are a people with an ancient legacy and a correspondingly long memory. If they sometimes appear prickly toward foreign criticism, it is because they spent a full century being abused at the hands of foreign nations – including our own. If at other times they appear overly proud of their accomplishments... can we as Americans really cast the first stone?

Our time in China was not long, but our Lord used it to teach our family some enduring lessons. I carry these lessons around with me every day, stored in a private note on my smartphone. Although some have been mentioned already in prior chapters, we gather them together here by way of summary...

First, having lived a charmed life beforehand, in going to China our family had the privilege to experience the pain of real sacrifice. To give up people, possessions, and a place we loved was not easy. But our Lord gave up far more for us. The sacrifices involved in going to China gave us a visceral taste of what our Lord embraced for us. Grace bears a bitter taste.

Second, having grown up as part of the majority culture in the United States, living in China gave our family a first-hand experience of what it is like to be an immigrant and minority in a foreign land. Although our status as American citizens afforded us certain protections, and though we were never mistreated, we also never forgot our different-ness.

Third, we learned that our true home is no place on earth. China was not our home, nor is the United States. Home is wherever God calls us to be and promises to be with us. Proximately, that may be in our country of origin or on the far side of the world. But ultimately, home is only that place where God will dwell with us: the better world of heaven and the new creation. Until we arrive there, we will always be foreigners.

Fourth, through the isolation of the mission field, particularly during our time when so many colleagues and friends had to leave, we learned to treasure friendship and community. Since our return from China, we have observed that many Americans seem to treat friendship lightly: easily acquired, minimally maintained, and readily replaced. Having lived in a place where friends were far less plenteous, we have learned the value of having people in your life with whom you have a mutual commitment to regular, deep communion. During our first four months in China, I was the only adult male on my team in Dongbei. I'd never felt so isolated – and this at a critical time when I was trying to figure out what it meant to lead my family in life overseas. Then my friend Jon made a commitment to call to me, via a secure channel, once a week. His friendship sustained me in ways I'll never forget.

Fifth, our security-necessitated isolation from indigenous churches taught us the value of being able to attend public worship services in a faithful church – without bringing danger to local Christians or risking deportation for ourselves. I wish I possessed the power to impress upon believers in Western countries just how tremendous a treasure this is. On the first Sunday after our return from China in summer 2019, my wife wept for the sheer joy of being able to attend public worship – with no fear of the police. What a privilege to possess this opportunity every week! What a shame to squander this opportunity even once!

Sixth, in leaving behind so many possessions in America, and then living in a smaller space in China, we learned that stuff is just stuff. The Lord showed us the danger of falling into the lie that happiness lies in the accumulation of things: houses, lands, clothing, entertainments, etc. We learned the value of having a low "stuff footprint" in this life.

Seventh and corollary to this, we were reminded of Western abundance and responsibility. For example, during our first months in China, I was asked to review a book. Published by a reputable Christian publisher, this book contained detailed exegesis of Messianic imagery in one of my favorite books, *The Lord of the Rings*. Because it was well written and the author presented a convincing case, I gave the book a good review. Nevertheless, from my vantage point, I could not help feeling a bit scandalized. There I was, living in a land where solid Christian literature was not easy to come by... and meanwhile, Christian publishers in North America were investing resources in "commentaries" on Tolkien. We must remember what Christ said: "Everyone to whom much was given, of him much will be required, and from him to whom they entrusted much, they will demand the more," (Luke 12:48).

Eighth, life in China has taught us that the scope of God's work in the world is always bigger than what we see in front of us. When we were living in China, we would remember people and places that we knew in America. Now that we are back in America, we remember people and places in China. In the summer before we left China permanently, it was very common for me to be sitting in my "home" in Pennsylvania, and then suddenly remember that I also had a "home" in Chengdu. Even a brief cross-cultural life tears off little bits of your soul and scatters them abroad. This can be painful, yes. But it is also a vivid reminder: no matter where you are, no matter what is in front of you, there is always more than meets the eye – somewhere else where life is also happening, some other place where people are living, smiling, crying, and sliding toward eternity. For believers in Jesus, it is a reminder that God's work extends well beyond the bounds of our peripheral vision. Life in China marked my family with a proper sense of the transcendent. May we never forget it!

Ninth, life in China enlarged my family's capacity for uncertainty – and thus our confidence in God's care for us. When you live with the constant possibility, however small, of an unwelcome knock at the door that could literally send you packing... you simply have to learn to live with more day-to-day uncertainty about your future. During our four months in Dongbei, every Saturday morning walk into the city to teach my illegal Bible study was an opportunity to remember: this could be the day when the study might be discovered and I might be detained. I learned a lot about real trust in Jesus during those walks. Those lessons proved useful to my family, even after we moved to Chengdu – and especially in the final months as local pressure increased.

Tenth, life in China taught us real lessons in humility and the crucifixion of ambition. There is nothing quite like learning a foreign language to teach you something of humility. And learning Chinese is hard! But I don't think that learning Chinese was the thing that taught us the most about humility. For my wife, I think the greatest lesson in sacrifice came with the decision to go to China in the first place. For myself, the greatest lesson in humility came with the decision to resign and return to North America. Why do I say this?

Throughout my life and labors, my motives have always been a mixture of sincerity and selfishness. Of course, I wanted to serve Jesus. But I also wanted to make my mark. As a church planter in those early years in Pennsylvania, who was to say that I could not be the next Tim Keller? In laboring overseas as a missionary, who was to say I might not make a contribution on the scale of John Calvin?

By removing us from China at a point where any contributions were modest at best, God confronted this ambition in me and helped me crucify it. Such humbling is always an ongoing process rather than a one-time event. Nevertheless, it was a strong beginning for which I remain thankful. In fact, if all of our life and adventures in China were for nothing else but this, it would be worth it. There is nothing in us so dark as selfish ambition, nothing so easy to ignore, and nothing which needs to die more. Thank God this is possible through Christ, in whom we can honestly say we have nothing to lose – and nothing to prove. The Lord did not need us in China, or anywhere else. In His story, our abilities and place are all only gifts of His goodness and grace.

Eleventh, through the whirlwind of events that took us to China and back again, we learned that God's providence is full of surprises. Not all of them are pleasant, but all of them are good. Yet even good decisions can carry a painful cost.

In addition to these lessons we learned on the field, my wife and I received some poignant advice before going to the mission field. Less than a month before leaving for China, in August 2017, a veteran missionary couple invited us for an overnight stay at their home. During the conversation that evening, they shared several crucial points of counsel. We append them here for the sake of all those who may someday take the cross to foreign lands – and for all those who pray for, send, and support them. My wife summarized their advice recently for another lady whose family was considering missionary service:

> 1) Missionaries should be Bible people first. You need to keep in the Word and seek Him in prayer regularly (if you're not already). Your relationship with the Lord needs to be your top priorty.

2) You and your husband both need to be on board. If one of you is unsure, then you either need to not go, or both work at being on board with the decision. It is so important for the husband and wife both to be unified on the decision. If one of you simply goes dragging feet, there will certainly be difficulties. To that, I would add that your marriage needs to be stable and in a good healthy place.

Regarding children, my wife summarized our friends' and our own experience as follows:

1) Try to get some sort of cross-cultural training before you go. Our family took part in a missions training program that prepared us well, kids included.

2) It's important to include your kids as part of the mission. Don't let it be just about "Dad and I are called" but about the family being called. We were encouraged to have our kids participate in whatever ministry we were a part of. For example, my husband taught free English classes as a form of outreach. We would bring our kids along to meet people. They enjoyed it, and the students loved having American kids there for conversation practice. Someone told me before we moved overseas (and he and his family had lived in China before as well), that children are more adaptable than you think. I was worried about the transition for them. I can't say that it wasn't without its hardships, but they did surprisingly well throughout our time there.

3) Routine. Establishing a good routine is so helpful when getting resettled. Kids know what to expect and what's expected of them.

4) Learning together. Before you go, learn all about the country you're going to: its culture, its language, as much as you can. When you finally land there, explore together. Take them to the local shops where you buy food. Have them practice speaking to people in their native language. Keep on learning the language and take lessons if you can.

5) Check in with them regularly. Ask how they're doing? How are they feeling? Especially with teens, as the transition may be hardest on them.

6) Make the home a safe place to be. Life on the outside will be unlike anything they've ever experienced, for sure. And it is good and wonderful and they should experience those things! But having a place they can return to, the home that you live in, helps them adjust.

My recollection of our friends' counsel mirrors my wife's – with one addition. As they shared their story, our friends emphasized that not everything had turned out as they had hoped. Yet despite some real sadness and difficulties, they would do it all over again.

So would we.

Conclusion:
Jesus Is Still Worth It

It was some time after our resignation from missionary service that my wife and I sat down with "Tom" and "Sue," friends of ours from our former ministry in Pennsylvania. At some point during our time together, Tom voiced the question that was on my own heart.

"So what was it all about? What did God want to do in you, that He had to take you there?"

Tom wasn't ignorant of all these lessons we had learned. He had read most of them in a letter I'd written some weeks prior. He was pushing further. What was the Lord's deep purpose?

I'd love to be able to tell you that we now know the answer to this question. But the truth is: we still do not know. There remains a large question mark in my mind over how our time in China fits into the main arc of our life story. This piece of our story doesn't make sense to me. Maybe it never will.

And yet, I can honestly say that we are not as bothered by this as some of our readers might expect. Yes, it would be nice if the ways of God always made sense to us. But if they did... would they still be the ways of God?

Before going overseas, we cherished a fierce love for certainty. We liked all of life's pieces to fit snugly together, with no jagged edges or nasty surprises. But life in China changed us.

215

Now, regardless of whether we ever learn the grand purpose God had in mind when He sent us to and from China – there and back again in less than two years, with all the sacrifices and sadness it entailed, and with the uncertainty it has unleashed – we are certain of three things.

First, quoting Jim Elliot, we say to all those considering missionary service: "He is no fool who gives what he cannot keep to gain that which he cannot lose."

Second, quoting Corrie ten Boom, we say to all those considering or recovering from missionary service: "Never be afraid to trust an unknown future to a known God."

Finally, we say to all what we said to ourselves at the outset and throughout: no matter what He asks or where He leads, Jesus was worth it.

Jesus is *still* worth it.

结束了

Glossary of Chinese Words & Expressions

Bàba (爸爸) father

Búhuìba (不会吧) "It cannot be possible!"

Chengdu (成都) capital city of Sichuan province; lit. "become a capital"

Dongbei (东北) the northeast region of China; lit. "East-North"

dōng-běi xī-nán (东北西南) east-north-west-south

ēnhuì (恩惠) grace

gǒuròu (狗肉) dog meat; a dish eaten in some parts of China

gǒuròu guǎn (狗肉馆) a restaurant specializing in *gǒuròu*; lit. "dog meat shop"

guānxì (关系) relational/social capital; lit. "connection system"

Guóqìngjié (国庆节) the Chinese National Holiday, one of China's *Huángjīnzhōu*

Huángjīnzhōu (黄金周) a week-long holiday; lit. "Golden Week"

jiāo'ào (骄傲) pride

jiǎozi (饺子) Chinese dumplings

kuàilè (快乐) happy, joyful

lǎobǎn (老板) shopkeeper; lit. "old board"

máfan (麻烦) — bother, hassle, inconvenience
mahjong (麻将) — Mahjong, a popular game using tiles
mànman lái (慢慢来) — "it takes time" or "take your time"; lit. "slow slow come"
miànzi (面子) — face; used in the sense of "saving face" or "losing face"
nánguā (南瓜) — pumpkin; lit. "south melon"
pàichūsuǒ (派出所) — a local police station/substation
píng'ān (平安) — peace; literally "flat quiet"
Pǔtōnghuà (普通话) — standard Mandarin Chinese; lit. "the common speech"
Qīngmíngjié (清明节) — Tomb Sweeping Day; lit. "Pure Brightness Festival"
Shèngjīng (圣经) — the Bible; lit. "holy Scripture"
Sichuan (四川) — a province in southwest China; lit. "four rivers"
Sìchuānhuà (四川话) — Sichuanese, a Chinese dialect spoken in Sichuan province
Sìgūniángshān (四姑娘山) — Four Sisters Mountain
suíbiàn (随便) — "as you please," casual, relaxed; lit. "adapt to convenience"
wàiguórén (外国人) — foreigner; lit. "outside country person"
wéiqí (围棋) — a game using black and white stones, called "Go" in the West
xiàngqí (象棋) — Chinese chess; lit. "elephant chess"
xiǎoqū (小区) — a Chinese apartment complex; lit. "small district"
xièxiè (谢谢) — "thank you"
xìn (信) — confidence, faith, trust
yángròu chuànr (羊肉串) — lamb kabobs; lit. "lamb meat skewer"
Yēsū ài nǐ (耶稣爱你) — "Jesus loves you."
Yēsū yě ài nǐ (耶稣也爱你) — "Jesus also loves you."
yílù píng'ān (一路平安) — "farewell"; lit. "peace on every road"
Yunnan (云南) — a province in southern China; lit. "southern clouds"
zàijiàn (再见) — goodbye; lit. "see again"
Zhōngguó (中国) — China; lit. the "Middle Kingdom"
Zhōngguórén (中国人) — Chinese person
Zhōngqiūjié (中秋节) — the Chinese Mid-Autumn Festival

Recommended Resources

Aikman, David. *Jesus in Beijing* (Washington, DC: Regnery, 2006)

Baugus, Bruce, ed. *China's Reforming Churches* (Grand Rapids: Reformation Heritage, 2014)

Fulton, Brent. *China's Urban Christians* (Eugene, OR: Pickwick, 2015)

Johnson, Ian. *Souls of China: the Return of Religion after Mao* (New York: Pantheon, 2017)

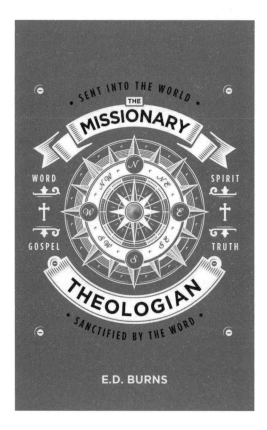

SENT INTO THE WORLD

THE

MISSIONARY

WORD

SPIRIT

N

NW   NE

W   E

SW   SE

S

GOSPEL

TRUTH

THEOLOGIAN

SANCTIFIED BY THE WORD

E.D. BURNS

The Missionary–Theologian
Sent into the World, Sanctified by the Word
E.D. Burns

- Importance of theology for mission
- For people beginning or in the middle of mission
- By experienced missionary

Gospel doctrine is the lifeblood of mission. Most missionaries in church history have prepared for the field with rigorous study and theological training, but there has been a move away from that in recent times. E.D. Burns contends that this is dangerous, leaving people ill–equipped to deal with the difficulties mission life brings. This brotherly plea challenges those who are already in, or are considering joining, the mission field to rest in Christ's work and abide in His Word.

ISBN: 978-1-5271-0539-3

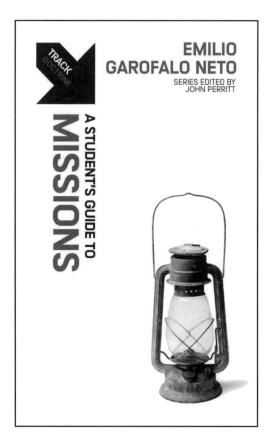

EMILIO
GAROFALO NETO

SERIES EDITED BY
JOHN PERRITT

TRACK
DOCTRINE

A STUDENT'S GUIDE TO
MISSIONS

Track: Missions
A Student's Guide to Missions
Emilio Garofalo Neto

- The importance of mission
- The place of mission in modern life
- From Track series for young adults

All of us have someone else to thank for receiving the good news of salvation. Mission is a means to a greater goal – God's name being glorified in the salvation of sinners. We should long to see God's fame being spread as far as possible. Throughout the Bible God chose to reach the nations through the preaching of His own people. Emilio Garofalo Neto helps us think through mission, the place it has in our world today, and our role in the mission of Christ.

ISBN: 978-1-5271-0896-7

Christian Focus Publications

Our mission statement –

STAYING FAITHFUL

In dependence upon God we seek to impact the world through literature faithful to His infallible Word, the Bible. Our aim is to ensure that the Lord Jesus Christ is presented as the only hope to obtain forgiveness of sin, live a useful life and look forward to heaven with Him.

Our books are published in four imprints:

CHRISTIAN FOCUS

Popular works including biographies, commentaries, basic doctrine and Christian living.

CHRISTIAN HERITAGE

Books representing some of the best material from the rich heritage of the church.

MENTOR

Books written at a level suitable for Bible College and seminary students, pastors, and other serious readers. The imprint includes commentaries, doctrinal studies, examination of current issues and church history.

CF4·K

Children's books for quality Bible teaching and for all age groups: Sunday school curriculum, puzzle and activity books; personal and family devotional titles, biographies and inspirational stories – because you are never too young to know Jesus!

Christian Focus Publications Ltd,
Geanies House, Fearn, Ross-shire,
IV20 1TW, Scotland, United Kingdom.
www.christianfocus.com